THE BLAC

Cover: The Wellington Monument

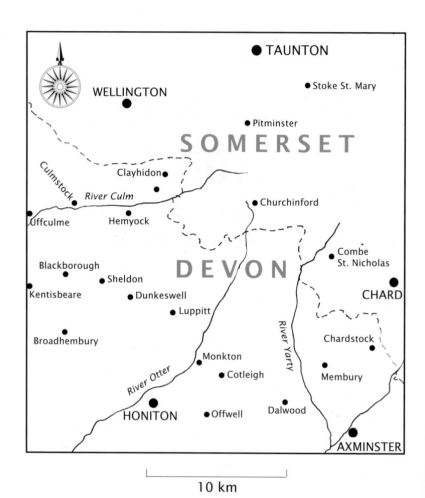

Sketch map of the Blackdown Hills straddling Somerset and Devon, drained by the Rivers Culm, Otter and Yarty, and ringed by the towns of Wellington, Taunton and Chard in Somerset, and Axminster and Honiton in Devon.

The Blackdown Hills

of Somerset and Devon

Shirley Toulson

EX LIBRIS PRESS

Published in 1999 by

EX LIBRIS PRESS
1 The Shambles
Bradford on Avon
Wiltshire
BA15 1JS

Typeset in 10 on 13.5 point Lucida Bright

Design and typesetting by Ex Libris Press

Printed by Cromwell Press, Trowbridge, Wiltshire

ISBN 0 948578 48 3

Contents

Author's Introduction

I have been fortunate in being able to spend some years talking with the people of Devon and Somerset; exploring the making of the landscape and the history of those two counties; and getting to understand their geographical and geological features through the soles of my boots. Naturally some aspects of the Blackdown Hills, where these two counties meet, have come separately into my two previous books. Now I feel very privileged to have had another chance to look closely at this region where Devon and Somerset meet Dorset and which belongs to itself alone.

For the Blackdown Hills are essentially their own place, a palimpsest of steep valleys threading wooded hills, the whole inter-woven with winding lanes which confuse and delight. The Blackdowns have recently been designated an Area of Outstanding Natural Beauty, which is a very fair description of the hills, although the bureaucratic label is a bit heavy for the contained countryside, which has the potential to offer a rare example of an organic lively community. The fact that those families who have lived in the Blackdowns for generations were wary of the designation, while in-comers welcomed it, speaks for itself.

As for me, I am, I suppose, a rank outsider, neither established inhabitant nor new settler, but I was able, when I had the happiness of living in Wells, to be a constant visitor. It is my hope that this book will prove useful to others like myself, who come to these hills, not as tourists bedevilled by the clock and their own preconceptions, but ready to discover and enjoy the experience of this part of England, which, in these days of mass uniformity, retains its rugged individuality.

I thank all the Blackdown people who have shared their enthusiasm for and knowledge of their hills, valleys, rivers, lanes and villages with me; and extend my gratitude to Richard Raynsford, a fellow-foreigner, who planned and accompanied me on so many Blackdown walks.

About the Author

Shirley Toulson worked as an education journalist and editor of the magazine *Child Education* until 1974, when she became a full time writer. Her first book commissioned by Shire Publications was a gazetteer of farm museums, still in their infancy at that time. Working on this led her to become fascinated by the links between agriculture and topography and eventually into following the routes taken by the drovers on their long journeys from the Welsh mountains to the English grazing grounds. This interest led to two books on the *Drovers' Roads of Wales* (published by Whittet Books) and others covering Derbyshire, East Anglia and the south-west peninsula. She is the author of *The Companion Guide to Devon* (Boydell and Brewer) and the volume on *Somerset* (Pimlico Press), published in 1995 in the County History Series edited by Christopher Hibbert.

1 The Lie of the Land

Where are the Blackdown Hills?

For the casual traveller between Somerset and Devon, the Blackdown Hills are simplified to define the spectacular ridge, adorned with the bayonet-shaped Wellington Monument, which marks the skyline to the south of the M5 between Taunton and Wellington. Should such a traveller take time out one day to leave the motorway at Junction 26, turn south again before reaching Wellington to cross above the streams of traffic and so climb up the southern escarpment to the crowning ridge, the real Blackdown country will start to reveal itself. For its folds of shapely hills, steep valleys and winding waters all lie to the south.

This is the Blackdown country that you will find if you turn west from Ilminster, leaving the A303 by the narrow lane that wanders up to the hill-top village of Buckland St. Mary. Here, as Richard Mabey so vividly described them in an article in *The Countryman*, the lanes become 'feral', an intricate maze that has evolved out of old drove ways and farm tracks, worn down between high-banked hedges. You must expect to get lost in the Blackdowns, finding your way by the sun and the lie of the valleys, for signposts are rare and often mutilated.

So, look north-west from the church at Buckland St. Mary to make out the valley of the Yarty, for if you want to reach the heart of Blackdown country, you must cross it, climbing through Bishopswood to the old ridgeway route that now carries the B3170 to Taunton. Across that road the land slopes

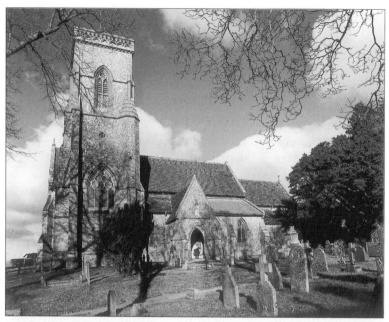

Above: Buckland St. Mary Church; Below: Valley of the Yarty.

down to the Otter valley and Churchinford. If you carry on west from there to Hemyock, just south of the River Culm, you will have some idea of the three major waterways of the Blackdown Hills. Happily we shall have good reason to explore them all, in some detail, as we look at the wildlife in their streams and valleys, and trace the human history of this self-contained country where Somerset, Dorset and Devon meet, and whose character is totally independent of those counties.

Should you go south from Ilminster to Axminster, and then turn north from the confluence of the Yarty and the Axe, the hills in the narrow valley of the lower reaches of the Yarty will present you with yet another aspect of the Blackdown Hills. It is defined by the rolling pastures that rise to wooded hill-tops, culminating in the ridgeway that runs north to south at the top of Stockland Hill. To the west of that hill, the land falls in a steep escarpment to the Umborne Brook. From Cotleigh on the other side of that valley, you can climb up to Monkton, where the A30 out of Honiton runs above the valley of the Otter to the west.

If you come towards the Blackdowns from Devon, you will find a third face to the hills, for this is altogether a wilder, harsher area, where narrow twisting lanes thread their way through conifer forests, patches of ancient woodland, heaths and wild marsh interspersed with fields of carefully tended pasture. Here, around Blackborough and Kentisbeare, there is an abundance of clay, and traces of old claypits which once provided the building material for the patches of cob that still remain in some of the older farm buildings. Recent proposals to exploit this on a large scale have been refused. In other parts of the eastern Blackdowns the loamy clay in the slopes below the greensand was used to make bricks; and in these western hills silica sand, also used in building, lies over the clay.

Stockland Hill

The Underlying Rocks

There is some iron-ore here on the Blackborough escarpment and in the lovely Bodiscombe valley to the north-east. Moreover, Blackborough boasts a greensand which really lives up to its name, for here stone composed of green glaucomite has worked its way up to the surface. It contains siliceans and until the end of the last century it was quarried for 'scythe stones' and used for sharpening agricultural implements in the same way that the Romans and the Celts of the hill-forts had used it to put a fine edge on their tools and weapons.

For the most part the greensand of which the Blackdown Hills are formed, and which is their dominant geological feature, presents itself as a hard, greyish white sandstone in which flinty, siliceous cherts are embedded. This chert is the natural building material of the area, and in the eastern part

12

you will often find it dressed with stone from the Ham Hill quarries near Ilminster.

The country we are exploring is based on the only extensive outcrop of Upper Greensand in southern England, and it is this that gives the Blackdown Hills their distinctive quality. The spring line, which occurs on the slopes of the hills, where this non-calcareous rock meets the much older Lower Lias (formed almost two hundred million years ago in the Jurassic era) and the Triassic Keuper Marl results in marshy meadows sloping down to the river valleys in which strata of the ancient rocks are exposed. These deposits of gravel and alluvium from the greensand and some overlying chalk were laid down by the river waters that excavated the landscape during the Pleistocene period, the most recent era of major geological change.

Beneath the spring line, the marshy ground culminates in extensive areas of peat stretching down to the valley floors. Until the end of the last century the Blackdown people had the prerogative of cutting this peat for their own use. This facility was known as the right of turbary and the name is still retained. The most significant are the turbaries in the Yarty valley and Ashculm Turbary in Hemyock parish, now part of a nature reserve and a Site of Special Scientific Interest (S.S.S.I.) where some important observations that we shall look at in the next chapter are being carried out. Dunkeswell Turbary to the west occurs on a plateau, but this is a rare phenomenon on the Blackdowns. It is well above the spring line from which the River Wolf rises to flow south into the Otter, just to the west of Honiton.

Millions of years ago, when the waters above the greensand subsided, deposits of fossil-bearing chalk were left. Clear evidence of this can be seen in such quarries as the long-abandoned working to the west of Membury church in the Yarty valley. Although the chalk, which is particularly predominant in the village of Whitestaunton and the hills to

13

the south of the A303, is not generally hard enough to be used as building material, its presence is sufficiently strong to affect the vegetation. In autumn, I have seen the alkaline-loving spindle blaze across the lanes around Pitminster.

In the eastern Blackdowns, there is also a certain amount of rough limestone above the lower lias. Some two hundred years ago, kilns were built on the hillsides here, so that the stone could be rendered down and used to enrich the poor, slightly acid soil above the greensand. You can see the remains of such kilns on the western edge of Thurlbear Wood, when we come to look at that hill-top nature reserve just south-east of Taunton on the fringes of the hills.

It is also in the east, at Snowdon quarry, another old working just to the north-west of Chard, that you can see most clearly how the accretions of chalk were laid down over the sandstone.

Staple Hill to the north-west of Buckland St. Mary, at the eastern edge of the main ridge, rises to 315 metres and is the highest point on the Blackdowns. Despite that modest eminence, the steep escarpment falling northwards from the ridge, and the steep slopes of the narrow valleys give the walker the impression of a landscape dominated by high hills and ridges. Some of the steep formations are due to geological faults occurring when the strata was displaced by movements in the earth's crust, which occurred in Britain about the same time as the upheavals that formed the Alps. One such fault can be traced from Sticklepath to the north-east of Combe St. Nicholas running past Snowdon quarry to the springline at Burridge to the east of Wambrook and Chardstock. Just to the west another fault has been traced from Weston Farm, by the site of the lost medieval village to the north of Wambrook. It runs to the east of the River Kit, a tributary of the Axe, and accounts for the sheer drop on that side of the valley.

Rivers

Like any other stretch of country, the Blackdown Hills are defined by the river valleys. In the east the watershed occurs on the ridge and from the spring-line around Staple Hill, whence Broughton Brook flows north to join the Tone. That river rises far to the west in the Brendon Hills and as it flows east across Sedgemoor to the Parret, it defines the northern edge of our area, as the Axe flowing south-west out of Dorset into Devon defines its eastern edge. The main river of the Blackdowns however is the Culm, flowing south-west from its source on the ridge, by the Holman Clavell Inn. Its valley is the main feature beneath the southern escarpment.

The Culm is the only Blackdown river flowing east to west, and its valley which runs almost parallel to the main ridge, is made up of wide, flat, water meadows, in striking contrast to the steep-sided narrow valleys gouged out of the hills by its main tributaries, Madford River and Bolham River, both of which flow north to south. The Culm flows for forty miles before emptying its waters into the Exe by Stoke Woods to the north of Exeter, taking a wandering course to its destination. Its very name is derived from the Welsh *cwlwm* (a knot) and indicates its true nature. Although it makes no abrupt change of course until it starts to turn to the south at Five Fords, half-way between Culmstock and Uffculme, and although its meanders do not appear very spectacular on the map, it is in a constant state of change, moving up to twenty of thirty yards from its previous bed after every flooding. In an attempt to control this movement, the old River Board followed the practice of putting boulders in the banks to control the floods. This proved fairly useless, and local fishermen complain that the boulders remaining from the last attempt at such control in the late 1970s are simply a nuisance.

Apart from its two main north-flowing tributaries, the Culm is joined by Hayward Water, which carves a fairly straight course down the hillside from its rising on the spring-line below Monument Farm and to the south of the road that runs along the ridge. It joins the Culm just to the west of Hemyock. Much further to the west, the Culm is joined at Cullompton by the Ken, rising from a spring just to the west of Kentisbeare.

The Yarty and the Otter are the major south-flowing rivers. The former rises south of Beeches Farm on Staple Hill and winds its way south-east through a narrow valley to Bishopswood. There it turns to the south, runs past Stockwood, where the valley widens into water meadows. It joins the Axe by the ruins of Remenham Abbey, south-west of Axminster.

To the west of the Yarty, the Otter rises by Yalham Farm to the north of Otterford and flows almost directly south past Churchinford, there it curves slightly to the west, passes through Upottery and the wide valley which came to provide the natural setting for a settlement at the junction of many ancient trade routes and which eventually became the lace-making town of Honiton. From there it leaves its Blackdown origins and flows into the sea by Budleigh Salterton.

The Yarty's longest tributary is the Corry Brook. It rises on the slopes of Broadley Hill, east of the A30 from Upottery, and flows past Millhayes and Dalwood to join the Yarty a mile or so to the north of its confluence with the Axe. Further to the west, the Umborne Brook, rising to the south of Upottery, flows south below Stockland Hill to merge with the Coly. The Otter's main tributary is the River Wolf. It rises by Wolford Lodge, to the south of Dunkeswell Turbary and flows past Awliscombe to enter the Otter just to the south-west of Honiton.

Water as a Resource

Many other lesser waters thread their way from the greensand spring line to the narrow valleys of the Blackdowns; and everywhere there is evidence of the way man has channelled this water, throughout the centuries, to make it serve his turn. There are traces of many old grain mills, and one working textile mill at Coldharbour near Uffculme; while Wessex Water and South-West Water both make full use of the springs and rivers to meet the need of the public water supply.

Coldharbour Mill.

During the early 1900s, Taunton Corporation Waterworks took some 600,000 gallons of Blackdown Water a day from a 500 metre tunnel bored into the upper greensand at Forches Corner at the eastern edge of the main ridge. The entrances to this tunnel, now carefully wired off, are bricked round on the wooded slopes of the nature reserve on Quants Hill.

Despite the size of the tunnel entrances and the elaborate brickwork surrounding them they are not easy to find, especially in summer, for they lie among the undergrowth to the side of the easily defined track running uphill from the ruined farmhouse of Quants on the lower slopes.

In earlier years many of the wealthier Blackdown estates organised their own water supplies. One mock-gothic waterworks of that period, now managed by the water authority, will confront you if you walk through Priors Park woods to the spring-fed valley to the east of Blagdon Hill. On the hillside to the west the little Blagdon reservoir has now been supplemented by the regular trapezoid of Luxhay Waters.

The reservoirs are not the only artificial lakes in the Blackdowns. Apart from the fish farms, fly-fishing which has always been a popular sport in the waters of the Culm, is now catered for in a more organised, commercial manner at various privately owned and stocked waters. For the most part such lakes are out of sight of the walker who delights in the natural flow of the rivers, but who may also take pleasure in the linear, wooded stretches of water that have been created out of the Otter to the south of Otterford.

2   The Life of the Land

Blackdown Mires

The predominate spring-line on the slopes of the Blackdown Hills, where the greensand meets the underlying rock, produces a wealth of mire vegetation, some of which is particularly characteristic of this region. During the summer of 1987, the Devon Wildlife Trust organised a survey, whose prime aim was to discover just how many Blackdown mires remain and how much they are at risk from agricultural drainage and other potential threats. It is still a valuable and relevant document. The mires, or wetlands, that the members of the survey team were looking at mostly consisted of areas in which peat has accumulated over the underlying mineral substrata. The wettest of these areas are characterised by sphagnum moss growing in hedgehog-shaped hummocks. Between them the surfaces of the swamps support sundew, and another insectivorous plant in the form of the rare butterwort. Liverwort flourishes here too and, more rarely, colonies of beak-sedge.

The Devon Wildlife Trust looks after two such areas of boggy land in Hemyock parish. One of them, Ashculm Turbary, stretches over seventeen and a half acres; it is a floating, high wetland on the western side of a valley, whose stream separates Hemyock from Clayhidon. This reserve was created a Site of Special Scientific Interest in 1976 and cleared some ten years later, enabling the bog asphodel to flourish and the ling and bell heather to emerge from the birch and alder scrub. Scrapings in the peat were made in the late 1980s, and this

Clayhidon Turbary.

has encouraged newts, dragonflies and demoiselles to make their homes here. Later on ponds were dug in the swamps, thus encouraging the spread of sedges and rushes. These ponds must be approached with some care, for although the quicksand areas have been carefully wired off, the ground around them is a quaking bog. Yet if you manage to peer at their shifting banks, you will see that these diggings show clearly how the chert underlies the peat. A similar area of turbary, owned by Clayhidon Parish Council, on the opposite side of the valley, contains similar valuable species, and is now being as carefully managed as the Ashculm site.

Fortunately Blackdown peat, unlike that of the Somerset moors, has not been exploited for horticultural purposes, for the narrow valleys make it hard to extract in sufficient quantities to be commercially viable. The main threat to these wetlands comes from over-drainage of surrounding pastures, one result of seriously over-stocking of the area, a matter which we shall have cause to look at in more detail later on.

The sloping meadow that makes up another Devon reserve beneath Dumpdon hill-fort just outside Honiton is characteristic of the wet pasturelands of the Blackdowns in their natural state. They are similar in many ways to the threatened Culm grasslands of north and west Devon, which have also been seriously eroded by over-stocking in the past years.

River Valleys

We must draw a distinction between these spring-line wetlands and the actual water meadows in the river valleys. Here the vegetation is quite different, and the bird life is typical of many rivers in the south-west. Dippers can be seen performing their curious bouncing dance on the rocks protruding above the surface of the water; and in the river banks, a keenly discerning eye can detect the holes in which kingfishers build their nests.

Culm Valley

There are still some otters in the Blackdown rivers, but since 1957, when the first litter of mink was born in the wild, they have been seriously threatened by these murderous creatures. The slaughter has been so extensive that the Culmstock Hunt has now turned its attention exclusively to trying to eliminate these animals. Even opponents of hunting, of which I am one, cannot be entirely opposed to this move. The Culmstock Otter Hounds, now concentrating on the mink, have the distinction of being the oldest such pack in the country. Their history goes back more than two centuries, and in the south transept of Culmstock church, a stained glass window shows William Collins the original founder of the pack. To its credit, the Culmstock Hunt abandoned otter hunting long before the legal restrictions against the sport came into force, and the pure-bred hounds which now scent

Water meadows near Hemyock.

out the mink are about as rare as the otters that their ancestors hunted.

Blackdown rivers have a bad history of pollution. In 1987 the Council for the Protection of Rural England described the Culm as the most polluted waterway in Devon; and at the end of 1980 a spillage of pig slurry into its tributary, the Madford River, caused such destruction that a fish farm had to be closed; despite that warning a similar spillage occurred nine years later. The Yarty is in much better condition and some salmon are still caught there. Yet modern farming methods, and in particular the disposal of nitrogen waste and the illegal pollution from detergents used in washing out dairies, continues to play havoc with the plant and animal life in the waters. Some species of fly have disappeared completely.

Heathland

Above the spring line there are also extensive heathland areas, such as the bracken and gorse-covered stretch of hill around Culmstock Beacon at the western edge of the main ridge. Apart from the gorse and whortleberries covering the thin, flinty soil, the main vegetation on the Blackdown heights is purple moor grass, while in areas of rough grazing you can hope to find colonies of the heath, spotted orchid.

Culmstock Beacon.

Wood and Forest

You are never out of sight of woodlands and conifer plantations in these hills; The Forestry Commission has planted acres of conifers all over the hills, and although this has resulted in a monotonous blanketing of the landscape in many areas, several plans for broad-leaf planting are well underway. These have been undertaken by the Commission itself, particularly in the Castle Neroche area, and by private landowners. You can see some immediate evidence of this in the pink, plastic sheaths guarding the saplings recently planted on each side of the M5 between Taunton and Wellington.

As well as that new planting, there are some areas of ancient woodland preserved and managed by voluntary organisations such as the Woodland Trust, which owns an area of apparently scrubby wood on the northern slopes of Sheldon Hill in the east of the region. Sadly however there has been no tree planting along the banks of the Culm for thirty years or more. This has had serious consequences, for as we saw in the last chapter, the rivers are liable to change their course every time they flood. On the other hand various organisations, such as the Blackdown Association have done their best to undertake some planting to replace the trees destroyed in the gales of 1990. One such area in which this new planting has taken place is on the top of Blagdon Hill, where oak, ash and ash interspersed with holly have recently been put in.

Nature Reserves

Woodlands native to the area are also encouraged in the nature reserves managed by the Somerset Trust for Nature Conservation and the Devon Wildlife Trust. These trees create their own habitats. For instance, on the higher slopes of the woods that make up Quants Reserve, the branches of the oak and ash trees support some rare lichens; and here as elsewhere in the mixed woodlands of the Blackdowns, there is a ground cover of dog mercury, amongst which you may find early purple orchid, broad-leafed hellebore and the delicately modest moschatel.

The reserves managed by the two county trusts are invaluable for the way they have preserved characteristic Blackdown habitats. To return to Quants, on the north-eastern slope of the main ridge, as well as its woodlands it also comprises some acres of rough grazing, so encouraging a vegetation that includes varieties of rushes and ferns as well as the expected purple moor grass and heath-spotted orchid.

To the west of Quants, the Somerset Trust manages another reserve in Castlefields, on the slopes of Wellington Hill, beneath the monument. There are some ruined farm buildings at the entrance to this reserve, but the management of this land has changed little during the last hundred and fifty years, and still corresponds closely to the pattern set out in the Tithe Map of 1839. Once again this reserve is made of a combination of woods and grassland. Dyer's greenwood, devil's bit scabious, sneezewort, purple lousewort and the spineless meadow thistle all flourish on the grasslands, which are grazed during the early summer months. The woodlands are mostly made up of oak, ash and maple, with some rare perched alder. They encourage a ground flora of bluebells and wood anemones as well as the expected, pervasive dog's mercury.

Early in the spring I have seen orange-tipped butterflies in the meadows of Castlefields, and indeed the whole Blackdown area attracts many varieties of butterfly. Several butterfly reserves have indeed been set up in the Blackdowns, but for obvious reasons they are not generally advertised. One that is available for walkers has recently been set up in the Forestry Commission's Buckland Wood below the Somerset Reserve on Quant's hill; and in the ancient Thurlbear Wood, the Somerset Trust has cleared glades so that butterfly-encouraging plants can flourish on soil enriched by the limestone. These sunlit open spaces are an enchantment of bluebells, primroses and violets; and as the summer months come, you will find silver-washed fritillary and white admiral butterflies here.

In the contrasting habitat of Devon's Ashculm Turbary reserve, I saw speckled wood butterflies in the cold, wet May of 1991. Martyn Winters, then warden of all Devon Trust properties in the Blackdowns, who took me to Ashculm Reserve and to the similar one on ten acres of land at Lickham Bottom, also in Hemyock parish, carefully encouraged those plants that provide a natural butterfly habitat. They include alder buckthorn, a shrub that only flourishes in wetland habitats, which provides food for the larva of the large acid yellow brimstone butterflies. The Lickham reserve is also notable for its covering of the pungent bog myrtle, a native of undisturbed wetlands and most vulnerable to drainage schemes. It is the host plant to at least two species of bush crickets.

As for the Blackdown birds, garden warblers and blackcaps, chiff-chaff, nightingales and woodpeckers all make their homes in the woods, and nightjars have been recorded on the Quant heaths. The Royal Society for the Protection of Birds has its own West Sedgemoor reserve of some thousand acres at Fivehead, to the east of the Blackdowns; and there you will find a hide from which to watch the comings and goings of eighty pairs of nesting herons, great birds that shake the quivering tops of the trees as they come back from their fishing grounds in the levels beneath the wood.

All these designated nature reserves, admirable as they are, should not detract our attention from the wild life habitats that are not officially preserved, but which are equally vital for the maintenance of a healthy and varied fauna and flora. Among such habitats, the hedgerows must stand high on anyone's list, and a balance has to be kept between what is

Above: Wood anenomes;

Right: Early purple orchids;

Below: Bluebells

best for a good, thick hedge and what is needed, in terms of bringing seeds, berries and nuts to fruition in order to sustain creatures such as dormice.

However, in the Blackdowns where most of the hedges are strongest in ash and willow this is not so much of a consideration. The main question here must be about the use of various types of mechanical hedge cutter, and that is a matter that the Devon Hedge Group is monitoring closely. Some people may even argue that the loss of a few of the hedges planted during the nineteenth century is not entirely bad news; for if the hedges go so do the mechanical cutters with their dangerous tendency to cause soil erosion.

It is such erosion, and the effects of excessive and piecemeal drainage that constitute the major threat to the character and wildlife of the Blackdowns. They are even more serious, being less reversible, than the pollution from nitrates and slurry that poison the rivers.

It is all a matter of balance; if the Blackdown Hills become an official agriculturally Less Favoured Area, it could mean that farmers would receive compensatory allowances for every head of livestock, an arrangement that could obviously lead to serious over-grazing. On the other hand, inadequate grazing of the meadows below the spring line, would mean that encroaching scrub would smother the sensitive mire vegetation.

We must remember that this is a man-made landscape, but that, at least, as we go into the twenty-first century, we are aware of what is at stake. In the next chapter I shall look at the history of the farming people and the landowners who have shaped the Blackdowns from prehistoric eras, and discover how they interacted with the life of the hills.

Robin Hood's Butts

3 The People of the Blackdowns

Prehistoric Settlement

The five tumuli, known collectively as Robin Hood's Butts, are the most spectacular evidence of Bronze Age Settlement on the Blackdowns. They flank the western edge of the B3170 as it runs along the ridge of Brown Down (whose name comes from the Celtic *bryn* – a hill) between the Otter and the Yarty. These tumuli are on private land, so one can only peer over the hedges at the shapely green barrows, which popular imagination at some time allocated to the hero of Sherwood Forest. How he found himself so far to the south-west must be another story.

The Bronze Age chieftains, buried here in shining chert-covered mounds that served both as monuments to the illustrious dead and as waymarks for travellers along the ridge, were not the first people to settle in the Blackdowns. There is plenty of evidence that Neolithic farmers flourished here, especially around Membury on the eastern slopes of the Yarty valley. There, their axes and finely wrought arrowheads have been found near the sites of Iron Age hill forts (inhabited some three thousand years later) and in the banks of such foxglove-lined green lanes as the one that runs from Millhayes by the Corry Brook to Stockland Little Castle.

The people of the New Stone Age were not the first people in the Yarty valley. Mesolithic hunter gatherers were here some ten thousand years ago, and left behind their delicately shaped microliths. Some of their axes have also been found at Crandons Cross by the river to the south-east of Stockland.

The Yarty was a natural boundary between Celtic tribes, which accounts for the hill-forts on either side of the river. It was these Celts who gave the Blackdowns their name. It comes from the Celtic word *blai* or *blag*, a wolf. Hence they are the wolf hills, a reminder of how important the stockaded hill-tops must have been as places for corralling cattle as well as serving as defence posts against human enemies.

Stockland Little Castle, whose earthworks were built by Celtic people, is a good example. The main entrance has been partly destroyed, nevertheless the circular enclosure, in which those early farmers kept their cattle safe from wolves and other wild beasts as well as human rustlers, is clearly defined. Here, as in many other Iron Age hill-forts in the Blackdowns, archaeologists have discovered signs of dwelling places and the remains of corn storage pits.

From the banks of Stockland Little Castle, you can look south-east across the valley of the Corry Brook to Beacon Hill and the peculiar hill-top formation (probably natural) known locally as the Devil's Frying Pan. Woodlands block out the view of Stockland Great Castle, less than a mile away to the south-west; and intervening hills hide Membury Hill Fort on the other side of the Yarty valley.

Should you cross the valley to seek out Membury Castle, you will find you can reach it by taking the lane and footpath from Membury church. That way you will come to the western entrance of a single ramparted fortress, 290 feet long and 100 feet at its widest part. This fortification stands on a steep spur of Upper Greensand covered in clay, flints and cherts. If you look south from here you can see the confluence of the Yarty and the Axe, and beyond those rivers to the coast at Axmouth and Seaton. From the junction of the rivers, a ridgeway goes past Membury Castle to Whitestaunton, Combe Beacon, and Castle Neroche on the Blackdown ridge, so forming an ancient north/ south trackway, which we shall look at again in Chapter 5.

Membury Hill Fort.

The major hill-forts in this southern part of the Blackdowns stand just to the north of Honiton. The A30 running from that town to Ilminster goes along the contour of the Otter valley. On the other side of the valley from the roadside village of Monkton, the beech trees that crown Dumpdon Hill Fort are a focal point in the landscape. The lanes wind up to the earthworks past Shaugh Farm, and if you follow them you will come first of all to the marshy meadow, now preserved as a nature reserve on the south-eastern slopes of the hill. It is separated from the outer ramparts by a beech-planted bank.

Flowers enhance the climb up to the hill-fort from that place, covering the banks with the gold of gorse and tormentil;

and should you have parked in the National Trust car park to the east, then you will find yourself walking up a steep, bluebell-covered hillside. Once you have made the climb, the reason for the siting of this hill-fort becomes immediately obvious. From here you can survey the whole Otter valley; and the hills of Devon, culminating in the granite plateau of Dartmoor, are spread to the west. Clearly this hill provided a good look-out post for warring Celtic tribes and one that must have been very hard to attack. There are several acres of flat grassland crowning its summit. They form a lush meadow and are surrounded by further enclosures to serve as a compound for the cattle, on whom the builders of this hill-fort depended. Furthermore, as the marshes of the nature reserve prove, the spring-line is not too far away, so those same cattle could be watered, and if necessary it would be possible to sustain a siege for some time.

However, it is Hembury hill-fort, a little to the west and standing at the end of a spur projecting south from the main greensand plateau of the Blackdowns, that has been claimed as the major hill-top stronghold in the whole of the south-west. If you take the path leading up through the trees to the camp, eight hundred feet above sea level, you will come to the Iron Age earthworks that surrounded the hill. They are only part of the story of Hembury. Archaeologists have found quantities of flint and chert artefacts here together with carbonized remains of wheat and barley, evidence that Neolithic farmers settled on this flat-topped height before 3000 B.C.

The Romans

The Iron Age Celts appear to have abandoned Hembury in the latter part of the first century B.C., but a hundred years later, the Romans made use of it, taking over the northern part of the hill-fort and restoring the Iron Age west gate. Evidence for the presence of the legions comes from traces of substantial timber buildings designed to serve as officers' quarters and as workshops. About 60AD the Romans left and the site appears to have been abandoned until the Middle Ages, when an annual November Fair was held here every St. Andrew's Day.

Hembury is by no means the only source of evidence for Roman occupation in the Blackdowns. The hills, after all, are not far to the north of the Fosse Way, the great highway which the Roman engineers surfaced and which ran across England from Lincoln to Axminster. In the 1840s, during alterations to the road that runs past the manor house of Whitestaunton, a village in the deep-valleys to the south-east, traces of a Roman villa were discerned. Forty years later, when the manor was occupied by Charles Elton, who was both a Q.C. and an M.P., the villa was partially excavated. It was obviously the

Manor House at Whitestaunton.

dwelling of a wealthy family, for it included living rooms, a sizeable bath-house, hypercausts, mosaic flooring, painted wall plaster, flue tiles, roofing slates and, best of all, glazed windows. If you go to Whitestaunton now and take the footpath towards Cinder Hill, you will pass rough swampy ground that shows rough signs of Celtic earthworks, evidence perhaps that the rich Romans could live peacefully beside the native tribesmen.

In 1914, Roman roofing tiles were found in the Yarty valley, in a field behind Membury Court Farm, close to the site of a thirteenth century chapel which I shall describe later. So, presumably, there was a villa there too. Then, in 1967, a tessellated Roman floor was uncovered in South Chard. When the Romans left Britain, the Celtic tribe of Dumnonia, which inhabited the Blackdowns, was saved by the impenetrable forests that covered most of the south of England, and by the steep hills and narrow valleys of their own terrain from the molestations of the Saxon hordes.

The Saxons

In 517 the Saxon Cerdic fought the Britons at a place called Cerdic's Ford, according to the *Anglo-Saxon Chronicle* and generally thought to be Chard; but it was not until the beginning of the eighth century that the Saxons finally gained dominion over most of the Blackdown Hills.

The entry for 710 in the *Anglo-Saxon Chronicle* informs us that in that year, 'Ine and Nun his kinsman fought against Geraint, king of the West Welsh; and in the same year Sigbald was slain.' Ine was the great Saxon king who had ruled Wessex since 688; and the West Welsh were the Celts of the south-western peninsula. The site of the battle is thought to have been either near Buckland St. Mary, or more likely Forches Corner, on the eastern edge of the northern Blackdown ridge (an ill-starred place whose name derives from the Latin, *furcae*, gallows). On a map of 1881, a Nun's Barrow is marked just to the west of that site, although the *Chronicle* does not indicate that Ine's kinsman fell in the battle. However, we know that Sigbald died, and he may well have been buried at Simmons Barrow, which lies to the south of the ridge by the main road to Hemyock.

Immediately after his victory, Ine built his castle at Taunton, and from there he would have controlled the eastern parts of the Blackdown Hills. The land to the west probably remained predominately Celtic for a long time. Most of our knowledge about land ownership and management in the centuries before the defeat of the Dumnonia and the coming of the Normans is to be found in the records of the Domesday Survey of 1086. From that we learn, for example, that Stockland in the Yarty valley had three mills, and that 'blooms of iron' were worked in the eastern part of the Blackdowns, notably at Cricket St. Thomas and at Whitestaunton. However, we must go back to the Saxon charters to learn who the main landowners were, and how the surrounding abbeys came to control so much of the best land of the hills.

It was in 958 that the Saxon King Ine gave the settlement that now carries the Norman name of Holcombe Rogus in the north-west of the area to the Abbey Sherborne; and during the reign of Edward the Confessor, the Bishop of Salisbury owned the arable lands, ploughs, mills and serfs of Chardstock. At the time of Domesday that latter estate was being managed by two knights, Walter and William. Stockland belonged to the monks of Milton Abbey, and the manor of Chard (Cerdie) which included two ploughlands, a mill and a herd of twenty-four nanny goats, belonged to Giso, Bishop of Wells.

Other lands were held by the Crown. They included the commons, woods and riverside meadows of Hemyock; while a Saxon charter indicates that the West Saxon king Aethelwulf had control of the lands at '*Stoc*, i.e. Stoke St. Mary. He was to give them to the minster church at Taunton. As the Anglo-

Saxon word *stoc* probably indicates a dairy farm or cattle fold, this was obviously a rich gift, but one that Taunton was only able to enjoy for some fifty years. For at the beginning of the tenth century, this flourishing estate was acquired by the Bishop of Winchester. During the Middle Ages it came back to Taunton Priory.

The Normans

As the Romans had taken over the Iron Age hill forts for their own purposes, so the Normans made use of Saxon earthworks and fortifications to defend their newly acquired lands and highways. Probably the most notable example of this in the Blackdowns is Castle Neroche, from whose height it is possible to look east over Sedgemoor and north-west across the Tone valley. Until the end of the thirteenth century this fortified hill-top was known as the castle of Raehich in the Forest of Neracchich (from the Celtic *rhac*, the spine of a hill).

The huge earthworks seem to have been thrown up by the Saxons in the middle of the eleventh century. A year after the Conquest, the Norman cavalry commanded by William I's half-brother, Robert of Mortain, seized it. Then a further series of four concentric ramparts were built, each one of which surrounded a courtyard or bailey. At the very highest point, on the edge of the hill, the Normans set their motte, and protected it by a deep ditch. It was crowned by a wooden tower, surrounded by a stout wooden pallisade. For some twenty years Count Robert used this castle as his residence, abandoning it in 1087, when he settled in the lusher pastures of Montacute to the south-east.

One of the best stories about land ownership at this time comes from Broadhembury, which still remains a feudal village, owned by the Drewe family. At the time of the Norman Conquest, this land was held by Brictric, a thane of Gloucester. He was foolish enough, in a worldly-wise sense, to refuse the advances of the infatuated Matilda, granddaughter of William I, later to become Queen of England. The story goes that it was the fury of that scorned woman that caused Brictric's rich lands to the west of Hembury Fort to be given to another half-brother of William I, Odo Bishop of Bayeaux. In the Middle Ages the estate was to come into the hands of Dunkeswell Abbey some six miles away to the north-east. So it was farmed by the monks until the dissolution of the monasteries in 1539.

Brictric was not the only Blackdown landowner to become impoverished when William I handed out gifts of land to his followers, partly as a reward for their services and partly to ensure a strong Norman presence that would keep Saxons under control. Many Blackdown place names contain evidence of the Norman families which once lived there. One example is the farm of Mohun's Ottery in the parish of Luppit. Its name comes from the Mohun who married Alice, a daughter of William Brewer of Dunkeswell. It was their son who built Newenham Abbey near Axminster in 1246.

The first infant Mohun to be born on the banks of the Otter may well have been christened in the font that still stands in Luppit church. Some people have suggested that this elaborately carved stone basin is the work of Saxon masons, but the general opinion is that it is early Norman. On each of its four sides it carries bold and lively motifs. That on the east face is said to represent the martyrdom of a local Christian saint by a pagan chieftain, perhaps a tribal leader from the hill-fort at Dumpdon; the north face carries a double-headed beast, a marvellous heraldic creature, a token of the evils of duplicity; the south face is secular, portraying a crowded hunting scene; and the west face is simply an exuberant celebration of woodland foliage.

Clayhidon, in the very heart of the Blackdowns, reached by Rosemary Lane which climbs up from the Culm to the main ridge, gets its name from the Hydon family. They were to become the first recorded lords of the manor of Hemyock, and traces of their hall still remain in the present house, largely built within the ruins of Hemyock Castle. Holcombe Rogus to the north-west is named for Rogo FitzNigel, a knight in the service of Baldwin, Earl of Devon, from whom he leased the manor.

These great Norman families were responsible for shaping the Blackdown landscape throughout the early Middle Ages, and for the building of abbeys and churches. Many of these are now lost to us, although several traces of their former widespread grandeur remain.

Among those ruins is a late thirteenth century chapel, now serving as barn, for the farm at Membury Court. It retains two of its original windows and part of a simple screen together with an intact piscina. The vestiges of a wide upper gallery projects far enough to the east to enable worshippers to look down into the sanctuary through the four-light squint of the wooden screen. Most of the information that I have gleaned about the chapel comes from a letter written to *Country Life* in 1957 by G.W. Copeland of Topsham. He claimed that Robert de Chandos gave the manor of Membury to the priory of Goldcliffe, on the Bristol Channel near Newport, which was founded in 1113 as a cell of the abbey of Bec in Normandy. So it was probably a French monk who served the community at Membury, a situation that was to continue until the suppression of foreign monasteries in 1414.

The Middle Ages

Dunkeswell Abbey to the south of Hemyock was also attached to a French order, that of the Cistercians of Citeaux. It was founded in 1212 by Lord William Brewer, Sheriff of Devon, before he became one of the triumvirate responsible for ruling Britain while Richard Coeur de Leon was in the Holy Land. Right through the Middle Ages the descendants of the original Norman landowners continued to build castles and to fortify their manor houses. On 5 November 1380, Richard II gave William Ascthorpe and his wife Margaret permission to fortify and crenelate, with a wall of stone and flint, the manor house at Hemyock.

Dunkeswell Abbey.

That order was made soon after the Black Death had wiped out about a third of the population of Devon. Indeed Margaret, who had inherited Hemyock Manor, was the sole survivor of a family of four children. It was a troubled time and William, her husband, appears to have been a short-tempered, quarrelsome individual. This was probably the reason why he was so anxious to apply for fortifications to his house.

In 1385, Margaret Courtenay, Countess of Devon, complained to the king that Ascthorpe had attempted to murder her steward, Henry Tyrell. She claimed that to accomplish that killing and to perpetuate further misdeeds, Ascthorpe had assembled forty malefactors at Hemyock for the purpose of attacking Henry Tyrell's house at Mersh (possibly the village of Marsh in the south-east of the region). When they arrived there to find that Tyrell was away from home, the rabble consoled themselves by beating his wife and setting fire to the house.

We do not know William's side of this lamentable tale, but we do know that in the previous year, when the abbot of Dunkeswell Abbey refused to pay his rents, Ascthorpe drove all the abbey cattle off his lands by the Bolham River and put them into a pound at Eynwardleigh. In that case it was the abbot who collected a gang of some fifty trouble-makers and rode at their head to attack his landlord's servants and release the herds.

People still talk of a secret underground passage linking Dunkeswell Abbey to the valley of Bodmiscombe to the west where there was a cell accommodating both men and women belonging to the Order of the Hospital of St. John. The land had been given to their Order by Henry Fitzwilliam of Sheldon together with Warin and Juliana de Aula who owned the valley. There are two farms in Bodmiscombe now, the original cell is thought to have been on the site of the larger one. It was apparently here, in the fourteenth century, that William de Quentin, vicar of Awliscombe (near Broadhembury) was apprehended as he tried to break into the cell. It is not recorded why he should have committed that misdemeanour, but we know that the offence was serious enough for the priest to be called to account before the King's court at Westminster.

The quarrels between the church landowners and the great secular lords reverberated through the villages that grew up in the Blackdowns during the later Middle Ages, when so many of the parish churches, such as that of Stoke St. Mary to the south-east of Taunton, were built. That church was linked to the more ancient church at Rushton, and belonged to Taunton Abbey which provided its priests from 1308. In 1963, the house where those priests lived was considered unsafe and demolished. Since the Reformation it had served its turn as a church house where meetings could be held and visitors entertained.

In 1243, William Brewer, Bishop of Exeter, gave the parish church at Sheldon to the Abbey of Dunkeswell, which enabled Abbot Ralph, some six years later, to make a private gift of Sheldon land and turbaries to Walter de la Hego. Ten years after that gift was made, Bishop Bronscombe of Exeter rode into the Blackdowns to dedicate the new parish church in Dunkeswell village to the south of the abbey.

Dunkeswell Church.

That village had been settled by the Saxons early in the ninth century. Its name may well come from a Saxon leader called Dunnoc. On the other hand it could simply refer to a well of dark water. For there is such a well on the hillside in the centre of the village. It is totally sealed over now, and not at all immediately obvious although it is just across the road from the village hall. Indeed when I set out to look for it nobody in the village seemed aware of its existence. Although it is so totally neglected, once as St. Patrick's well it was closely linked to the history of the village, for all that the church is dedicated to St. Nicholas. The Patrick of the well, was probably not the saint of Ireland, but Petroc, a sixth century Welsh monk, who crossed the Bristol Channel into Cornwall, and who, together with his followers, settled many Christian communities in the south west.

However, by the fourteenth century, the villagers of Dunkeswell knew the well as St. Patrick's; but as they drew their water from it they were probably quite as indifferent to its origins as their successors, who rely on a mains water supply, are today. The villagers of the Middle Ages were kept far too occupied by the labours involved in wresting a living from a harsh and difficult land to bother about history, as they supplemented the contents of their larders by hunting and poaching in the hills.

Much of the land of the Blackdowns was then reserved for the Crown. The Royal Hunting Forest of Neroche covered many acres of the eastern hills, and to the south a deer park formed part of the estate of Chardstock. In that parish, Robert Hyndely was appointed park keeper in 1432. It was apparently a post worth holding, for as well as access to the game, it brought in 2d a day, and the choice of 6s.8d. or a robe each Christmas.

By the thirteenth century weekly markets were being held throughout the region. In 1218, the Bishop of Sarum gave permission for such a market to be held in Chardstock; it took place in the square in front of the present George Inn. This market was one of many to be granted either by the King or the lords of the church; but important as the weekly markets were in the life of the Blackdowns, they were a small adjunct to the great annual livestock fairs. The one at Chard brought the outside world to the Blackdowns. Welsh black cattle were shipped across the channel to Minehead and then driven south to that fair where they were interspersed with the native shaggy red Devons. More local fairs were held at important river crossings and intersections of highways. One such was held at Stockland, where the right to hold a fair was secured in 1268.

Dalwood to the south had to wait until 1345 before Edward III granted its right to hold a fair at the time of the feast to which the parish church was dedicated. As this was a St. Peter church (probably another corruption of Petroc) the feast was held in June.

In most cases the fairs were closely linked to the parish church. They would start with a service and procession on the eve of the Saint's day to whom the church was dedicated and continue for a full three days. Something of the splendour that must have attached itself to the ecclesiastical processions that preceded the fairs can be judged by looking at the pre-Reformation cope that is now kept on view in Culmstock church. Heavily embroidered, it dates from the late fifteenth century, and must have been hidden away to save it from the depredations of the Reformation. It was later cut up to serve as an altar cloth. A Christ in Majesty was depicted on the cowl, while the centre of the cope showed the Virgin surrounded by angels. The border consists of a series of magnificent panels, each one devoted to a saint, an apostle or a martyr, all standing in complex architectural settings.

Although the religious processions ceased with the Reformation, the livestock fairs were still being held in the nineteenth century and played an important part in the development of agriculture in the region, as well as incidentally establishing the routes of the major highways. these are matters that I shall look at in the course of the next two chapters.

Forde Abbey.

4 Shaping the Land

The Reformation

The Blackdowns that we know today began to be shaped when Henry Vlll ordered the dissolution of the monasteries in 1539. Then the church lands were parcelled out among wealthy families, who set about building great mansions on the sites of former abbeys and emparking their land. The Cistercian Forde Abbey, on the eastern fringe of the area and now open to the public on certain days of the year, is a prime example. When its abbot Thomas Chard together with his twelve monks handed the abbey over to the king, they left a splendid and magnificent building. For Thomas had devoted most of his energies and resources to it since he became abbot in 1521.

Turned out of Forde, he became vicar of Thorncombe to the south of the Axe, a parish outside our area. Strictly speaking Forde is too, although it must be included in any study of the Blackdowns because of the extensive lands the abbey held in the hills, and because of the effect that its post Reformation owners were to have on the history of the area. Dunkeswell, in the heart of the Blackdowns, was to suffer a worse fate than Forde. After the Dissolution it became a virtual quarry for the building of farms and houses in the area. One of its monks, John Gaye, was appointed as parish priest of Sheldon with a stipend of six guineas. His rector and former abbot, John Ley, had charge of both Sheldon and Sainthill until he became vicar of Payhembury in 1557.

It seems that the parishes as well as the private landowners may have benefited from the Dissolution of the monasteries and abbeys which freed so many able people to take their part in the community; although the Blackdowns must have had their share of impoverished, mendicant and resourceless former monks. It was about this time that the so-called Priest's House was built at Holcombe Rogus. Now in the care of the Landmark Trust and available for holiday letting, this building was probably originally a church house, serving as meeting place and inn for the parish.

Priest's House at Holcombe Rogus.

Age of Elizabeth I

Towards the end of the sixteenth century, Edward Drewe, Sergeant at Law to Queen Elizabeth I, built a great new house at Broadhembury, on the site of the former Dunkeswell Abbey barn. It was to remain in his family for more than 300 years. Nationally the sixteenth century was a time of great expansion, and this was reflected in the Blackdowns as yeoman families like the Drewes, as well as the great landowners, began to amass their fortunes, largely through the burgeoning wool trade and its allied textile industries. This was when the weavers of Chard became established; and other processes linked to clothes manufacture, such as tanning, received a fresh impetus from the new wealth. It was indeed to a tanner, William Chace of Membury, that the Court in the Yarty valley was leased by the church landowners in 1550.

Post Office and Stores at Broadhembury.

As England grew richer, the threats from foreign powers became stronger. In June 1569, a muster of men and weapons was ordered throughout all Devon villages. The parish constable had the duty of drawing up lists of all able-bodied men and their weaponry, the arms, for the most part, being provided by the landowners. Seventy men were included in the muster list for Hemyock, they included two members of the Bowreman family, who lived at Whitehall Manor on the north bank of the Culm to the east of Culmstock. Lawrence Bowreman had a pike, a hand pistol, a helmet and a corselet; while Andrew was listed among the archers.

The threat from Spain was to end with the defeat of the Armada in the summer of 1588; but in the months leading up to Drake's victory the fear of a Spanish invasion was acute. For an early warning system, piles of firewood were built up on the hill-tops, so that they could be lit as a signal of the approach of the enemy. Above Culmstock a small round hut, built of chert from a hill-side quarry, was erected. It still stands there, a building with a single 'window' and a hole in the roof, in which a fire would burn brightly whatever the weather. If you walk up to it now, making your way through gorse and heather, you will observe, if the day is clear, what a magnificent viewpoint this is. The watcher on this hill would easily be able to see when the fires were lit on the Dartmoor tors.

One positive effect of the misery of the Spanish wars was the start of the chair trade which was to flourish at Holcombe Rogus, Burlescombe and Uffculme into the mid-nineteenth century. It is thought that the local craftsmen learnt the art of making these simple, straight-backed chairs from Spanish prisoners of war.

Civil War

Fifty years after the defeat of the Spanish Armada, the country was torn by the disaster of Civil War. A look at the fortunes of some of the parish vicars shows how the national tragedy was brewing up in the Blackdowns. John Pitt, a vicar of Chardstock, who became warden of Wadham College, Oxford, in 1644, was dispossessed of that post five years later for his part in denying the authority of the Parliamentary Commission. The next year he was ignominiously turned out of his own vicarage by James Strong, a poor tailor of Chardstock, who worked 'for a groat a day, his pottage, bread and cheese.' Strong's action was particularly harsh, because, way back in the 1630s, Pitt had befriended Strong and sent him to Oxford where he became a scholar at New Inn Hall. Benefiting from that education, Strong was eventually to be nominated by Oliver Cromwell as a 'publique preacher' in Ilminster.

Like most of the rest of the country, the Blackdowns were divided in their allegiance once war broke out between king and parliament. Many of the landed gentry were on the side of the king. Francis Bluett, whose brother John had inherited the manor of Holcombe Rogus in 1614, was killed in the Royalist cause at the Siege of Lyme Regis in 1644. Sir John, like the vicar of Chardstock, was connected with Wadham College, Oxford, founded by Nicholas and John Wadham of Branscombe, on the coast of east Devon, so it attracted much local support and interest. Before hostilities broke out, Sir John presented the college with a gold flagon, which was shortly to be melted down to provide the desperate Charles I with cash.

The Spekes of Whitelackington, the Hills who lived at Poundisford Park and the Popham family of Hemyock Castle were staunch Parliamentarians. Although William and Lucy Hill, who substantially enlarged the original early Tudor house in the late sixteenth century, were proud to display the Royal Arms of the Protestant Queen Elizabeth and in 1603 to entertain Anne of Denmark, James I's queen; by the time of the Civil War their descendants' allegiance was to Cromwell. Roger Hill became Member of Parliament for Bridport in 1645, and later sat in the Long Parliament. A lawyer, he was to become a Baron of the Exchequer, and he was named in the commission for the trial of Charles I. However, he was so successful in disassociating himself from the regicide that Charles II had no hesitation in knighting his son after the Restoration. Yet, while the war was going on, Hill was such a threat to the Royalist cause, that, in 1645, Goring's troopers raided Poundisford Park in order to lay hands on his documents before they rode off to the siege of Taunton.

Hemyock Castle was used as a prison for captured Royalists at the beginning of the Civil War. In March 1643, the King's troops, led by Colonel Francis Bluett of Holcombe Rogus, attacked it. They took the castle on the 9th of that month and captured the whole of Hemyock the next day. There were at that time two hundred prisoners in the castle, among them was James Burnard, a former rector of Awliscombe and Upottery, who had shown himself sympathetic to the king's cause. The Pophams' resistance to the Royalists was so strong that, after the Restoration, Charles II ordered that Hemyock Castle should be slighted. The Civil War was accompanied by outbreaks of the plague which ravaged many towns and villages throughout the country. Hemyock did not escape. In the one month of June 1646, 57 people are recorded as dying from the fearful infection. The survivors, together with many other people in the west country, were mindful of the suffering that the Royalist army had inflicted on Taunton, and peace did little to ease the bitterness of this memory. When the monarchy was restored in 1660, these people became active Dissenters from the King's Anglican church and twenty-five years later they were eager to support the avowedly Protestant Monmouth in his bid for the throne of his uncle James II, rightly suspected of being an under-cover Papist.

The result was a tragedy that over-shadowed the bloodshed of the Civil War, and in which nearly the whole of Somerset was engaged. It ended in the fearsome slaughter of the Battle of Sedgemoor, which was followed by the vindictive mass executions ordered by the dyspeptic Judge Jeffreys. Christopher Bathscombe, one of Monmouth's men in Brussels, who came to the Blackdowns for a secret meeting with George Speke of Whitelackington before the Duke landed, was one of the more prominent men to die at Jeffrey's order. Most of the victims were village lads, frightened at the thought of more

Hemyock Castle.

powerful landowners under a Papist regime. Edmund Prideaux of Forde Abbey, who had entertained Monmouth during his progress through the west country, was imprisoned in the Tower of London, but saved himself from the gallows by paying a fine of £15,000. Whereas, Charles Speke, also of Whitelackington, who refused to swear against Prideaux was hung at Ilminster, a reprieve arriving too late.

St. Mary's Church, Hemyock.

Agricultural Change

Meanwhile, apart from the tragedies of war, the reshaping of the medieval landscape continued throughout the seventeenth century. Early in 1630, despite opposition from Lord Poulett of Hinton St. George, who had been a head forester since 1619, parts of Neroche Forest were enclosed. The parishes of Ilton, Barrington and Whitelackington were still able to enjoy the common grazing rights for a further two hundred years over much of the area, but by 1631 a substantial acreage had been enclosed for the growing of wheat. It is strange in these days, when we think of the destruction of hedges as a crime committed by greedy farmers that, in the seventeenth century, the landowners were protecting them from agricultural Luddites. From Chard, we have a record showing that a certain Richard Luffe was paid ls. 8d (about two and a half days' pay for a farm worker at that time) for whipping three hedge breakers.

As new agricultural improvements, which included the planting of these quick-set hedges came into force, lime-burning to enrich the soil was being undertaken in the lime-rich eastern part of the area. Most of the lime-kilns that you see in the hills date from this time. So do many of the old orchards, for it was in the seventeenth century that cider began to replace beer as the main farm brew.

Lime kiln at Bishopswood Meadow.

At the same time as such agricultural changes were taking place, the cloth industry continued to flourish. Spinners and weavers, carders, tailors and clothiers are all listed in village records, and field names such as Tuckers and Fullands indicate where cloth working was prevalent.

Life of the People

Partly as a result of the Civil War, the more general conflicts between the New and the Old Religions, and above all because of the subsequent plague, the seventeenth century saw an upsurge of superstition and witch-hunting throughout the country, a phenomenon that was not confined to the uneducated. The Blackdown Hills were not immune. In 1656, the corporation of Chard found it essential to pay out the sum of 19 shillings in order to have a new ducking stool to try old women accused of witchcraft; in 1684, Richard Bovet, a native of Wellington, published his *Pandemonium or the Devil's Cloyster*. In it he quotes the story of the man from Combe St. Nicholas who fifty years previously had come across a band of little men returning from the pixie fair. These small creatures, clothed in red, blue and green, were said to frequent the Blackdown Hills between Pitminster and Churchinford. It seems to me that we have evidence here of the isolation of the hills, as a result of which their inhabitants kept themselves apart from their richer neighbours and could even become belligerent to the people in the surrounding lowlands. Perhaps the 'pixies' had been to the fair at Hemyock to which outsiders were not welcome. Certainly it was considered unlucky to let the pixies know that you had sighted them.

After the tragedies of the seventeenth century, it is small wonder that the people of the Blackdown Hills became somewhat indifferent to church affairs in the years that followed. Stoke St. Mary was not the only church to have an absentee rector, although in that case, the Reverend Charles Russell must have held a record by leaving his church to a succession of curates for a matter of sixty-five years, only returning to his parish when a dispute about the tithes arose. A notable exception to this general indifference to spiritual matters may well have been found at Broadhembury from 1768 to 1778, at the time that Augustus Montague Toplady was vicar. He is the author of the hymn, 'Rock of Ages,' which he composed whilst sheltering from a thunderstorm in a crevice of the crags of Burrington Combe on the Mendip Hills.

In the Blackdowns, the Age of Reason was at least marked by some mitigating social concern, such as the attempt to meet the needs of the poor by providing some rudimentary education in such institutions as the short-lived House of Industry, established by the rector of Hemyock in 1785, which was dissolved in mysterious and distressing circumstances seven years later. At the same time a start was being made to improve roads and communications in the area, a matter that I shall look at in more detail in the next chapter. This work was largely undertaken by trusts made up of the great landowners, who spent much of their wealth in enlarging their fine houses and emparking their land.

The Napoleonic Threat

By the end of the century, threats of a foreign invasion once more affected the Blackdowns. Detailed plans were made to collect all the cattle together and to drive them as far inland as possible, so that foreign troops would find it difficult to obtain provisions. Clayhidon Hill was fixed as the assembly point for the herds in that large parish, according to a pronouncement made in May 1798, which added that waggons, carts and horses should also be assembled there, reaching the place by means of Holly Lane, Rosemary Lane and Bar Park Lane. From Clayhidon they were destined to go east to Castle Neroche and Ashill on their way to the wide valley grazing grounds beneath Somerton.

The commander of the troops in the south-west was

General John Graves Simcoe of Wolford Lodge near Dunkeswell, who in 1795 had just completed a three-year tour of duty as the first Lieutenant Governor of Upper Canada, the present day province of Ontario. Back home, he established an emplacement of two hundred guns on St. Cyres Hill, manned by men from Luppit.

These French wars, like all others, increased the cost of living for everyone, and for most people on the Blackdown Hills the last years of the eighteenth century were lean. Matters were made worse by the weather and in particular the very wet summer of 1799, when the cost of wheat rose to a guinea a bushel. On 22 February 1802, before the Napoleonic wars were over, General Simcoe and his wife Elizabeth consecrated the chapel at Wolford, which they had built on the site of an earlier church where, in the seventh century, Wulfhere, the first Christian king of Mercia, founded a settlement in Wessex. When his successor Ethelbald came south he built a church here and dedicated it to Wulfhere's memory; his name lives on in Wolford. Four years after the present church was dedicated; having been taken ill en route to become commander-in-chief in India, General Simcoe was buried against the east wall. He actually died in the home of the Archdeacon of Exeter, his funeral procession making its way east to a torchlight ceremony at the chapel, now in the care of the Ontario Heritage Foundation. It is open to the public although it stands in private grounds.

R.D. Blackmore, Author

In 1825, the novelist R.D. Blackmore was born at Culmstock, where his father was the curate-in-charge. Best known as the author of *Lorna Doone*, this writer, prevented by epilepsy from following his career as a barrister, wrote, towards the end of his life, a novel about the Culm valley of his boyhood. *Perlycross* is the Culmstock he knew and the title of the novel, in which his father appears as Parson Penniloe. Here he recalls his fascination, which visitors can still share, with the yew tree that grows out of the church tower. His book is by no means a purely rural idyll, for he gives us a description too of the quarrying for the sharpening stones then being undertaken around Sheldon to the west.

Coming of Industry

While R.D. Blackmore was still a boy, steam was starting to be used to run the woollen mills of Chard, which were rapidly being converted to the making of lace, an industry in which some fifteen hundred people were employed by 1830. Many of the workers went daily through the arched entrance to the five-storeyed mill, recently put up by Messrs. Boden, whose name is immortalised in that street. About the same time an iron-making business was set up in Chard by John Wightman working in partnership with Charles Dening.

In 1836 a Union Workhouse was established in the town. It was to last more than a century, although two years after it was opened the *Chard Union Gazette* declared it to be an inefficient erection already delapidating'. By 1851, the census returns show that there were 219 paupers in the Union, most of them being local farm workers together with unemployed sail and cloth makers from Crewkerne.

Lace making was still one of the main Chard industries, and it grew throughout the century. In 1826 there were 49 bobbin lace makers in the town, thirty years later their number had grown to 360. In 1874, the Amalgamated Society of Operative Lace Makers set up a lodge in Chard, over-riding a prohibition written into all apprentice agreements about joining or supporting a union. Industrial action was taken by the employers in December 1878, when a lock-out was imposed because the unions had opposed a reduction in wages. It continued until February 1880. Among the lace makers, was William Bondfield, born in 1814, the son of a cloth carrier. His daughter Margaret, born at Furnham near

Chard in 1873, where she was to become a pupil teacher at the Board School, went on to become a trade union worker in London and eventually the first woman cabinet minister and privy councillor.

The town industries became an essential source of work and income as enclosures altered the face of the countryside and the amount of common land diminished. The hedges came fairly late to the Blackdowns, creating several new farms particularly in the eastern part of the region. In West Buckland parish a total of 781 acres were enclosed in 1815; and five years later under the enclosure act of 1816, of which the Duke of Wellington was the chief sponsor, 355 acres of land to the north of Wellington, including the hill on which the monument now stands, was enclosed. This land was eventually to form Monument Farm, where you must now collect the key if you want to venture up the narrow stone spiral staircase to the top of the monument. Although some common lands remained around Corfe, Pitminster and Otterford up to the middle of the century, much of it was lost when the Taunton Enclosure Act of 1851 parcelled up 2,430 acres of the eastern hills.

The Nonconformist Influence

Throughout the century, small voluntary schools, such as the one in Clayhidon set up in 1824, became generally prevalent; and as industry increased and the skills of literacy were more generally available, the non-conformist movement spread into the hills, and was welcomed by people long-neglected by many of the parish churches. In Stoke St. Mary an Independent or Congregational chapel was built in 1825 on land given by a man and his wife aptly named Weaver. It soon had a flourishing congregation made up of labouring families, who in 1849 went off to hold open-air mission meetings in Stoke Woods where the hills echoed to the sound of hymns sung by three hundred people.

Stoke St. Mary Congregational Chapel.

Their religious fervour was partly occasioned by the fearful poverty of the 1840s. Those who wanted urgent temporal reform in preference to some heavenly bliss took to the streets demanding food. In 1874, George Braddick of Heazle Farm, Clayhidon, was attacked by a mob on his way to Taunton with seventy pounds of butter. He took refuge in a house a mile out of the town, but the rioters, led by twenty-two year-old John Phillips, burst open the yard door and took his horse, cart and butter into the market place. There the butter was sold at a very low price to the starving people.

In 1849, the parishes were for the first time authorised to appoint full-time paid constables, but recruitment was not easy and many of the applicants could not read or write. The parish stocks were still in use as a means of punishment.

Despite the refurbishing and restoration of the parish

churches during the latter part of the nineteenth century, often at the expense of the original medieval fabric; the non-conformist movement continued to flourish in the hills, confirming its beginnings. In 1827 a license had been granted for the holding of a Wesleyan meeting at Ashculm, and the Methodist chapel was built in Hemyock nine years later. When the Baptist church held its first services in the town on 24 October 1865, two thousand people attended in the morning and three thousand in the afternoon. This religious fervour was to culminate in the evangelical Blackdown Mission, founded in 1860 and still extremely active.

The history of this mission has been written by Ronald H. White, a Blackdown man born at Bolham. It was published under the title of *Strength of the Hills* in 1964 by the Paternoster Press. The mission was founded in 1859, by George Brealey, born at North Tawton in Devon on 4 September, 1823. By the 1890s, chapels were established at Rosemary Lane, Bolham, Stapely, Sheldon, Culmstock and Browndown, the latter eventually being moved to Bishopswood where it still flourishes.

The enthusiasm for the spreading non-conformist sects was not entirely confined to the labouring classes and the poor. At Poundisford Park in Pitminster, the Welman family, who had lived in the Tudor mansion since the beginning of the eighteenth century, became devout members of the Countess of Huntingdon's Connection, a group of Calvanistic Methodists with strong Welsh connections. The Pitminster Welmans built the chapel at Fulwood to the east, and it can still be reached by a footpath curving round the edge of the park. The well-known hymn, 'I think when I read that sweet story of old' was written by Jemima Luke, a connection of the Welmans, who taught at Blagdon Sunday School, where it was first sung.

As in the other parts of England, the Blackdown non-conformists were, for the most part, a practical people, with the welfare of working people close to their hearts, and they were furnished with sufficient common sense and business ability to be able to do the best for them. In 1885, in the depths of the agricultural depression, four non-conformist farmers from Hemyock set up a co-operative creamery. It started as the Culm Valley Dairy Company and was based at the Mountshayne farm of Mr. J. Clist, one of the founders. In those early days the butter was stored in an underground cellar and the skimmed milk from the process was fed to pigs, a regular pig market being held at Millhayes. This was to be the first firm in the west of England to produce butter mechanically, and the first in the world to use milk collected from the dairies only once a day. It also looked to the future by encouraging the children of local farmers to rear calves in order to improve the milking herds. From that scheme the Young Farmers' Clubs had their beginning. Seven girls and twelve boys, all with shorthorn calves, started the scheme.

Despite all this modernisation, the old superstitions persisted. When Mrs. Cook of West Buckland became too blind to earn her bread as a weeding woman, she was taken to Wellington workhouse. She left behind a cottage chimney blocked by a bullock's head stuck full of pins.

As late as 1910, blackened stumps of wood blunted the scythes of the reapers reaping by the earthworks of the hill-fort on the flat-topped Beacon Hill to the south of Stockland. Still known locally as the Devil's Frying Pan, this is said to be the place where effigies of unpopular people were burnt on ground where witches had been tied to the stake.

As at Glastonbury, a very early flowering hawthorn grew in the Blackdown hills at Whitestaunton and West Buckland, and people would come from as far afield as Clayhidon to see it flower on 5 January, the date of Old Christmas. F.W. Matthews, who wrote on the Blackdowns in 1923, had to admit that by that date the West Buckland hawthorn was 'a not very imposing bush'.

Beacon Hill.

Blackdown Artists

When Matthews' book, *The Blackdown Borderland*, was published, the hills were becoming known to the world at large through the work of three artists from the Camden Town Group who came down to Applehayes in Clayhidon parish in the years just preceding the 1914 war. In the latter years of the nineteenth century, Applehayes farm was owned by a gentleman from Monkton near Bath. After he had sought his fortune in Argentina, he went to the Slade where he met Frederick Spencer Gore, and in 1909 brought him to the folded hills above the Culm. Gore must have been enthusiastic about the scenery he found there, for he was soon joined by his friends and fellow-painters, Charles Ginner and Robert Bevan.

The latter, whose unsentimental, almost architectural landscapes are the best known of the three, was so happy painting in the Blackdowns that, in 1916, he bought a cottage in Bolham Water, and immortalised that river in one of many pictures of the neighbourhood. He also left a record of Culm bridge and its mill as they were in his day and an evocation of an evening in the Culm valley, which is timeless. Charles Ginner, who lived on until 1952, left a record of Gollick Park Farm, Clayhidon. It is still virtually unchanged. From these paintings, we have some idea of farming in the Blackdowns in the first part of the twentieth century, when the ploughing matches organised by the Clayhidon Agricultural Society stipulated that no furrow could exceed nine inches in width or be less than five and half inches deep. In those days the judges were not simply devising exercises of skill to impress the visitors, but consolidating farming techniques.

Modern Times

It was all to change, after two world wars and the mechanisation of agriculture had altered the face of farming throughout England. We shall look at this in the next chapter, when once again it will become apparent that the Blackdown Hills are an area of their own, and must be given special consideration although their character was already beginning to change in the years between the wars. That was a time of intense agricultural depression, people moved away from the hills in search of a living and the village populations rapidly declined, leading to the loss of the local schools and small businesses.

The first impact of the second world war was the arrival of the London evacuees from East and West Ham; but this 'safe' area was not entirely immune from Hitler's bombs. In June 1940, the second bomb to be dropped in Somerset exploded near the Nag's Head in Stoke St. Mary, and in the following year the neighbouring Thurlbear church was damaged by one of three parachute mines that fell in the area.

When America entered the war, a branch of the U.S. Navy Fleet Air wing was stationed at Dunkeswell for two years. In the parish church you will find a memorial giving the names of those who were killed while flying from this bleak plateau, among them is that of President Kennedy's brother, Joe. The original tower of Dunkeswell church was damaged by vibrations during the two years that Liberators and Catalines were flying from this base. It had to be totally demolished in 1947, and the present tower dates from 1954. In 1965, the U.S. Navy presented the parish with a new organ, an assurance that the people of Dunkeswell in future generations will remember the American presence in their village.

5 Roads, Canals and Railways

Roads

The earliest trackways in the Blackdowns, like those everywhere else in these islands, went along the ridgeways, and of these routes the most obvious example is, of course, the Blackdown ridge itself. Along this ridge the Celtic and Saxon leaders moved their armies towards the decisive encounter at Forches Corner. But in this territory of steep narrow valleys there are many other ridgeways as we have discovered; and several of them run north to south like the one that keeps to the hill-tops along the east of the Yarty valley, going past Wambrook and the ridge known as the Half Moon by Membury and over Haddon Hill towards Axminster, while to the west of the river a road runs along Stockland Hill. Further west again an old road ran across the plateau of Dunkeswell to Uffculme.

Soon after 43 AD, when the Romans pushed their way south-west towards the estuary of the Axe, and engineered the Fosseway, running diagonally across England to Axmouth from Lincoln, they made use of many of the old routes used by Stone and Bronze Age people as well as by the Celtic tribes. So in following that great road as it runs through Chard parish, we shall come across signs of much older thoroughfares that linked up with it. The people who lived in the villa at Whitestaunton were probably familiar with the ancient highway that runs north towards Taunton from the Fosseway and skirts the Blackdown Hills to the east.

From the time that the Roman legions left until the setting up of the Turnpike Trusts, hardly any road making was undertaken in the Blackdowns or anywhere else in England. During the Middle Ages travellers simply used the most convenient and the driest routes linking one river crossing with another, and in many cases these followed the drove routes or the tracks along which farm produce was brought to the fairs and markets.

A look at some of the river crossings will give you an idea of the routes taken by these roads, a particularly good example being Beckford Bridge, a single-arched pack-horse bridge that crosses the Yarty and links the present metalled lane leading up to the Membury ridge to the east with the footpath that goes south-east to Dalwood. Another indication of the medieval farm tracks are to be found in the still existing green

Beckford Bridge.

lanes running from the hill farms to the sites of the old water mills by the rivers. One such will take you across Lemons Hill, to the south-east of Hemyock, to the mill at Bolham Water.

Many of these farm and market ways were used for military purposes during the Civil War, and it was either by going north along Hemyock High Street as you enter the village from Honiton or east along the present Culm Bridge road from Ilminster that the Royalist soldiers marched to capture the castle for the king.

With the coming of the enclosures, some routes such as the Driftway, originally known as the Long Droveway, across Chard Common, were left as access roads. At that time the roads throughout England were still practically non-existent. The old tracks, some of them gouged out into hollow ways and all of them deeply rutted were quite incapable of carrying the increased traffic of carts and coaches. Gradually the Turnpike Trusts, set up partly as an investment by the great landowners, began the expensive task of surfacing the major highways. It was the first engineering to be done on the roads since the time of the Romans.

The unpopular tolls that were introduced to pay for this work were not a totally new imposition on farmers and travellers, for there had been a toll gate on the Stockland road from 1555; but the widespread introduction of charges was a heavy burden to face, and wherever possible old lanes were used as a way of avoiding the tolls.

The Chard Turnpike Trust, set up towards the end of the eighteenth century, was responsible for forty-five miles of local roads. These included five miles of the London road over Windwhistle; the main Axminster road; Perry Street; the Taunton road as far as the present Eagle Tavern, with an off-shoot to Holman Clavel; and the ten and a half mile road to Honiton. The latter more or less followed the course of the present A30 to Yarcombe. On Snowdon Hill the toll house still stands where two of the three daughters of the toll-keeper carried on their dressmaking business.

On the Axminster road out of Honiton, the toll gate still stands beside an unusual crenelated toll-house. On the road from Chard to Taunton there was a gate at Crimchard and a further gate near Deadman on the slopes of Staple Hill. The Turnpike Trusts were responsible for setting up milestones. They varied in design. In the case of the Chard to Axminster road they took the form of triangular stone pillars on to which cast iron plates bearing the information were fixed.

River bridges as well as roads had to be strenuously maintained and protected. At Longbridge to the north-east of Stockland on the road to Chard (once part of the route taken by the London to Exeter coach) a notice was posted on the bridge in 1770. It protected this crossing of the Yarty by declaring that anyone 'wilfully injuring the County Bridge will be guilty of felony and liable to be transported for life.' The same dire warning can be read on the single-arch nineteenth-century bridge in Stockland village.

In our own time the greatest change in the roads around the Blackdown Hills has been the construction of the M5. It takes most of the traffic to and from Exeter away from Honiton, and so keeps the hills happily cut off from casual visitors, who often pass by without being aware that they have come anywhere near the Blackdowns.

Canals

At the end of the eighteenth century, when the Turnpike Trusts had already done much to improve communications through the country, it became apparent that the cheapest way of moving goods from one place to another was by canal. To the north of the Blackdowns an ambitious scheme was devised for linking Taunton and Exeter by means of a canal whose course would run above the Tone. This scheme was incorporated into an Act of Parliament in 1796.

In fact the canal was never to go further than Tiverton.

Now the section running east from the Devon border is almost lost, although enough traces of it remain to provide an interesting walk for canal detectives, who can still just make out the site of its course, and speculate on the various devices for winching and lifting the short tub boats from one level to another. These small boats had been developed by James Green, who became surveyor of Bridges in the County of Devon in the 1830s; and in hilly country they proved infinitely more manageable than the conventional narrow boats.

West of the Devon border there is still water in the canal, which together with its tow path has been made into a County Council Country Park, offering pleasure rides in horse-drawn barges as well as towpath walks. If you take such a walk you will find as you go west from the county border that the canal winds beneath the great stone quarries at Westleigh. On the east of the ruined mill by the remains of Canonsleigh Abbey on the northern banks of the canal, you can still see the earthworks marking the route once taken by the rails running down to the quay, still discernible on the canal-side. Here the stone was loaded on to waiting barges.

In 1834, the Chard Canal Company was launched and the necessary Act of Parliament gave its plans the go-ahead in the June of that year. You can still see the facade of the Company offices in Furnham road to the north-east of Chard centre. It took eight years for the thirteen-and-a-half-miles of the canal to become fully operational. It was designed to carry goods to the Taunton-Bridgwater canal, and the water to fill its locks came from the newly dug Chard Reservoir. The course of the canal to the west of this sheet of water was too steep for conventional locks, so once again use had to be made of James Green's small tub boats. They were manoeuvred into cradles and moved up and down the single track by means of water-powered wire turbines. The engineer responsible for this intricate working was Sydney Hall, a young man of twenty-two.

71

Above: Earthworks for rails to canal side (Westleigh);
Below: Remains of quay on canal at Westleigh.

In the same year that the Chard Canal Company started operations, the Bristol and Exeter railway was opened, so extending Brunel's Great Western Railway into Devon and running eight passenger trains a day as well as two good trains along its whole length. For a while this left both the Trustees of the Turnpike roads and the Canal Companies unaffected in the southern Blackdowns, for the railway came no nearer to Chard than Taunton.

That was not to everybody's liking. Indeed on 14 November 1851, William Dommet, a Chard solicitor, councillor and former mayor arranged a public meeting in Yeovil to demand a central railway line going through Chard and linking the towns of Honiton, Axminster, Crewkerne and Yeovil. His appeal was unsuccessful and it was not until 1867 that the railway finally came to Chard and the days of the Turnpikes and the canal were over.

Railways

Meanwhile the northern part of the Blackdowns had always been served by God's Wonderful Railway, for Brunel's Great Western ran through Taunton and Wellington to Burlescombe and Tiverton, for the most part following the course of the Grand Western Canal which it soon rendered obsolete. The most substantial feat of engineeering in the construction of this line was the Whiteball tunnel in the hills to the east of Burlescombe. Today in the hill-top church of that village you can read some doggerel lines penned by the novelist R.D. Blackmore (a great railway enthusiast) commemorating its building.

This stretch of the railway served both the Westleigh quarries and the chair makers of Holcombe Rogus, whose goods were sold throughout the country until the early 1900s. Above all the railway was to alter the character of the villages along its course, for now it became possible for people to live in the country while working in Wellington, Tiverton or

Taunton. By the time the station at Burlescombe was closed in 1965, the car had made commuting a general and common practice, and opened the Blackdown Hills to waves of incomers, few of whom were in any way reliant on the area for work.

At one time this was a state of affairs that the people living in the central part of the Blackdown Hills would welcome. On 7 February 1899, the Parish Council of Clayhidon passed a resolution demanding that the Culm Valley Light Railway, a seven-mile branch line from Tiverton Junction to Hemyock (whose course can still be traced by Culmstock bridge) opened in 1874, should be extended to the east. They argued that 'from its picturesqueness and (owing to its high elevation) the unusual healthiness of its climate, the district would, if provided with railway facilities, in all probability become a favourite place of resort,' and so urged upon the Railway Companies the desirability of extending their services in accordance with the wishes of the inhabitants.

The Blackdowns are quite accessible now, although they will never be on any well-beaten track, and how much the inhabitants of Clayhidon and the neighbouring parishes really welcome this change, we will discuss in the next chapter.

6 The Blackdowns Now

Agriculture, Industry and Conservation

The Blackdowns are primarily an agricultural area, and so it is the farmers who are mainly responsible for the shaping of the landscape as we go into the twenty-first century, as they have been throughout history. In 1860 the farmer who bought Culm Pyne, built a magnificent mock-Tudor farm house on the site of the Culm Barton holding recorded in the Domesday survey. It stood on chalk land, which the new owner regularly flooded, creating water meadows by an intricate arrangement of ducts and sluices that drew the water down from the 650 foot spring line.

Culm Barton fields, like much of the other agricultural land of the Blackdowns, was not enclosed until 1837, and so the hedges are on the whole of no great age. Removing some of them would not be the historical and ecological tragedy that it has proved elsewhere, for this has never been easy land to farm, a fact acknowledged by its recent listing as an Environmentally Sensitive Area, a status that does not please everybody on the Blackdowns.

The objections are partly economic. Mr. Stallard, who has kept a dairy herd and grown corn and kale at Culm Pyne for the past forty years feels that any farmer, who accepts the conditions laid down with the E.S.A. grants, is going to be hamstrung by restrictions. For unless inflation should start to hold at zero, they will find themselves committed to undertakings at continually rising costs. Some farmers, like Bob Hill, decline subsidies (which are not index-linked) and make a virtue of 'dog and stick' farming, managing their land with a minimum reliance on machines and expensive artificial aids.

Culm Pyne.

Mr. Stallard, on the other hand, is determined to move with the demands of the time; and in common with many other farmers in the south-west, he is cutting down his dairy herd, and looking for alternative uses for his land. In his case his plans are centring on the planting of cider orchards. That change of use emphasises the close link, some would claim identity, between agriculture and industry. In that sense, as farming in the Blackdowns has always been difficult, much of the land has for long been given over to more directly industrial uses; as the conifer-clothed hills bear witness. Now the crops of soft wood are grown almost entirely for pulp; but in the early years of this century, long before the Forestry

Commission came into being, farmers were planting their land with firs for pit props to be used in the Somerset and South Wales coal mines.

Land use is always linked to patterns of employment, and the present decline in dairy farming, which Mr. Stallard accepts as inevitable, has made one of the greatest changes in the employment prospects in the Blackdowns. When the Honiton Milk factory closed in January 1992, because of the E.E.C. restrictions, one hundred and thirty people were made redundant.

The rate of change may be accelerating, but an agricultural landscape is never static. Shelford, in the western hills, originally had four farms, whose names can still be traced on current maps. They were Eastcott, which has long been the site of Sheldon Manor; Westcott; Southcott; and Northcott. Since the nineteenth century houses have been built all over the old fields, so now around Sheldon, you will find a mixture of late Victorian middle-class mansions, plastered bungalows and red-brick suburban dwellings. Even such farms as remain, here and elsewhere throughout the Blackdowns have substantially changed their nature. At one time every farmer had to give up some ground in order to grow food for his cattle; now he buys it in from the animal food manufacturers, such as Sheldon Jones in Wells, thus creating a further strain on the Blackdown lanes.

That strain is reflected in the controversy over one stretch of Blackdown land that has not been farmed for half a century or more. I refer to the Dunkeswell plateau, which the Americans used as an air-base in World War II, and which has since been given over to various light industries. In 1989, a developer wanted to use the site as a car racing track and general leisure and sports complex. He envisaged the installation of a large luxury hotel and at least one golf course. Immediately the residents in the parishes of Dunkeswell and Sheldon set up an action committee to oppose the scheme.

They were not simply objecting to the desecration of the plateau itself, but to the inevitable construction of the two-lane feeder roads that would be needed to service such installations.

In March 1992, the District Council approved a further development plan for Dunkeswell, which would permit hangers to be built on the edge of the airfield. However, they added a proviso that such hangers should be used for aircraft only, thereby frustrating any plans to turn them into a nucleus of industrial or leisure activities. This scheme was defeated and there is now a sizeable industrial estate on the old airfield.

Traffic and Tourism

The clogging of the roads has, however, already happened around Westleigh quarry, worked by Tarmac and English China Clay. Since both the canal and the railway closed, the road stone has had to be carried away in great lorries for which the Blackdown lanes were never designed.

These quarries, once used almost entirely for providing building stone and lime for the fields, have always affected the character of the countryside. In the early 1900s, so many workers were needed that quarrymen came in from Cornwall and South Wales to settle in Westleigh. Some of their descendants stayed on but the stone-taking is now done almost entirely by machine. As in so many country areas, tourism is becoming one of the main Blackdown industries, and many farmers are taking advantage of this. They let their cottages out to holiday visitors (a trend that began at the turn of the century); they plant crops of tents and caravans on their fields; and they provide bed and breakfast accommodation for the passing motorist who has strayed off the beaten track. To keep some of these people holidaying in the area, fish farms, stocked with trout for visiting anglers have been set up.

The idea that the life of the Blackdowns should be swamped by holiday visitors in the same way that the tide of tourists

flood into most of the rest of Devon, is repellent to many people. Indeed, it was because they feared that the whole character of this remote area would be altered, and that at best the hills would be turned into some sort of museum piece, that so many of the people living in the Blackdowns resented the recent designation of the place as an Area of Outstanding Natural Beauty.

Area of Outstanding Natural Beauty

Many farmers fear the restrictions that they are bound to encounter as they come up against the new regulations, and they resent the implications of becoming a 'snapshot in time.' Even the members of the Blackdown Association (founded in 1982) who worked with the Countryside Commission towards obtaining the A.O.N.B. designation, were wary of the unwelcome, tourist-based commercial interests that the new status might attract. On the whole, however, they feel that the grants made to the farmers, working in an area declared Environmentally Sensitive would ensure that the land was worked, at least, as it had been since the mid-twentieth century. As we have seen, there is no general agreement among the farming community that this will be, or should be, the case. In fact, when he confirmed A.O.N.B. status on 370 square kilometres of the Blackdown Hills, Michael Heseltine, then Minister for the Environment, had to over-rule objections from the National Farmers Union.

The nationwide Ramblers Association was, however, delighted that this range of hills with 'its beech woodlands, its intricate network of hedgerows, its meadows, heaths and beautiful villages' would be preserved for walkers who enjoy the countryside.

Here as elsewhere it would seem that there is a great divide between the farmers and the conservation lobby, in which the Ramblers Association must be included. That is to take too simple a view of the matter. There is at least one outstanding example of a farmer aiding the preservation of the natural habitats of the hills and positively aiding the work of a conservation trust. To retain the natural meadows at Woodend Farm near Bishopswood on the upper reaches of the Yarty, the farmer sold 23.5 acres to the Somerset Trust for Nature Conservation for a mere £35,000. Unfortunately this generosity has to be offset by the destruction caused in other places by over-intensive farming, and in particular by over-stocking land with pigs. This can cause extensive areas of former meadow to be churned into acres of irredeemable mud. In a newsletter for January 1992, the Somerset Trust claimed that Ringdown Common, within the A.O.N.B., had lost 85 acres to damage by pigs. This is very wet acid bog land, and the Trust claims that had they been able to buy it ten years ago, it would have become one of the best nature reserves in Somerset, but that it is now virtually irreclaimable. That instance of pig damage is not the only one on the Blackdowns, although it may well be the most ecologically destructive. For long stretches of the year I have found that the lane that runs north/south off the ridge to the west of the Wellington Monument has been rendered impassable to the walker by the slurry accumulating from the vast numbers of pigs folded in the neighbouring fields, now rendered barren.

Like every other stretch of English countryside, the Blackdowns will always be the scene of conflict between those who, at one extreme, have little concern about long-term depredations and who look on any stretch of land as material for immediate, possible gain; and those, at the other, who would attempt to freeze the processes of change, even to the extent of controlling and over-managing the course of nature. As always there is a middle way; it takes a lot of hard thinking and hard work to arrive at it, but the people I have met who are truly concerned for the preservation of the identity of the Blackdown Hills, are prepared for that.

Loughwood Chapel.

7 Chapel, Sangha and Church

Loughwood Chapel

It is no surprise that an area as remote as the Blackdowns should be the home of some of the stricter non-conformist sects. From the seventeenth century there has been a congregation of Baptists here, and the Strict Baptists still have a considerable influence in the hills. Back in 1668, twenty years before the arrival of the tolerant William of Orange, a Baptist minister wrote from Exeter gaol to inform a friend that 'They at Dalwood have a very large and increasing meeting.' They met in the Loughwood chapel, which since 1970 has been under the care of the National Trust, who have beautifully preserved it, replacing the roof slates with reed thatch as had been the case in the seventeenth century.

At that time the Baptists meeting at Dalwood found themselves frequently at odds with the local people. Many Baptists worked in the cloth trade, and it is quite likely that their hard and honest work, coupled with their simple living, infuriated their more profligate neighbours. So, although at one period the Cromwellian regime would have allowed them to worship in peace, they chose to meet in a chapel transformed out of a remote cottage in dense woodland, which could only be crossed by narrow tracks. Another great advantage of the site was that it lay then on the border of Dorset and Devon. So it was possible, when the persecutions of non-conformists became stringent under Charles II, for the minister and his flock to escape into whichever county seemed safest when the alarm went off that the chapel might be raided.

Loughwood is one of the oldest Baptist chapels in England. The woodland is thinned now, and a lane runs by the chapel, but it is still a lonely place. Services are still held here, but they do not last for the whole of Sunday, as was the case when the early Baptists met in this remote spot. They would have ridden through the woods from farms and villages throughout the Blackdowns and from along the coast of East Devon. They brought their food with them, the men eating in one room, the women in another. During the service they sat in pews, whose high partitions made it impossible to see anyone but the preacher; and they baptised their converts and young people by total immersion in the spring-fed tank below the pulpit.

Meeting House at Spicelands.

Quakers

While the Baptists were defying the State at Loughwood, the Society of Friends were settling into their brick-built Meeting House at Spicelands, a farm to the west of Culmstock. Originally built in 1670 and restored in 1815, this Meeting House, where Quakers have come together for over three hundred years, stands in the farm garden and can be visited by arrangement. Here you can see a copy of the deed granting the building to 'the people of God called Quakers' prominently displayed.

The Church in the 'Godless' Blackdowns

Despite such pockets of sanctity and good sense as Loughwood and Spicelands, by the early nineteenth century, the Blackdown Hills were on the whole fairly wild and godless. Like much of the rest of the country, the established church, totally dominated by the gentry, had little to offer ordinary people; while most of the parsons regarded their work as a sinecure and gave their time to other pursuits. One rare example was Ellis Williams, curate of Clayhidon, who worked to bring the Gospel to the people by holding prayer meetings in his own home. In 1790, he died at the young age of thirty-two, and for a further sixty years, Clayhidon was almost entirely neglected by the church. There as elsewhere in the Blackdowns, in places remote from the main thoroughfares through Devon and Cornwall, lawlessness, violence and disregard for the fundamentals of human decency were all too often rife, shocking polite society which did its best to ignore its less privileged neighbours.

Blackdown Hills Mission

That was the situation in 1863, when George Brealey, an evangelist, born in North Tawton on the edge of Dartmoor came to Clayhidon, having renounced his plans to emigrate to the West Indies in favour of a mission field nearer home.

By 1865 he had launched his Blackdown Hills Mission and opened Clayhidon Chapel. The Mission still flourishes in several of the original chapels, notably in Rosemary Lane and Bishopswood. In the initial stages of his work, George Brealey was helped by Charlotte Hanbury, daughter of a wealthy family that lived in 'The Firs' on the ridge by the Wellington Monument. She took it on herself to tour the area in a covered waggon, giving news of the Mission to outlying farms and hamlets. In 1869, George's son Walter gave up his London job and came to the Blackdowns to open the first Mission school. For over a century the Brealey family led the Blackdown Mission, George's grandson, David, being in charge for the 1963 celebrations. The Mission continues to play an important part in the life of the Blackdowns, drawing faithful and lively congregations to its chapels. It has done so for decades.

Mr. Henry Sparkes, who until his retirement in the 1980s, farmed Field Farm in Clayhidon parish , which his father took over in 1906, told me with pride of the prize which he had won in 1917 when he attended the Blackdown Mission chapel in Rosemary Lane. He made it clear that throughout his life, the teachings of the chapel had been his main support. A full account of the Mission has been recounted in *Strength of the Hills*, written by Ronald White, George Brealey's nephew, at one time vicar of Stoke Fleming near Dartmouth. It is tempting to wonder how George Brealey would have welcomed the advent of a Buddhist community to a cottage near Upottery.

Buddhists

As I write, there is no doubt that the nuns of the Devon Vihara at Odle Cottage, Upottery, are part of the established spiritual life of the Blackdowns.

In this small area of steep valleys and isolated farms, the twin forces of establishment and superstition that were once so dominant are giving way to the concerns of the material world and the new search for spiritual values. Here, in an area which has nurtured two Archbishops of Canterbury (both Frederick Temple, brought up at Axon Farm near Maidendown, and his son William had connections with Culmstock); and where gangs of pixies were alleged to threaten travellers returning home late at night, a new sense of order is emerging. It is coloured, of course, by the numbers of incomers, now that the car has made it possible to live in the Blackdowns and work in Taunton, Wellington and Exeter. Perhaps these days are coming to their close. It may well be that in another generation people will have to live where they work. When that happens the Blackdowns may once again be a remote and highly individual area.

Gazetteer

This Gazetteer of places in the Blackdown Hills is in alphabetical order. Each name is followed by a map reference. All are featured on Ordnance Survey Landranger Map No. 193, unless otherwise stated. Cross references to other entries in the gazetteer are indicated (q.v.).

Applehayes 174155
A footpath runs over the hill from the inn at Clayhidon to Applehayes Lane, which goes over the crest of the hill to Garlandhayes. As you walk west to east above Applehayes Farm you look over the landscape which drew Frederic Spencer Gore, Charles Ginner and Robert Bevan to come and paint in the Blackdowns during the early years of the twentieth century. They were all members of the London-based Camden Town Group, and were first introduced to the Blackdowns in 1909 by the then owner of Applehayes Farm.

Ashculm Turbary 145159
The footpath, that runs west from Simonsbarrow and then turns south at 153147, goes round two sides of this Devon Nature Reserve, a designated Site of Special Scientific interest stretching over 17.5 acres of high wetland. Access to the reserve can be arranged through the Devon Wildlife Trust.

Axminster 295985
The Roman Fosse Way, now the A358, which forms the south-eastern boundary of the Blackdowns, runs past the market

town of Axminster. There was a settlement here before the Saxons infiltrated the west country, so when Alfred's son, Athelstan, established a college of priests here, it served a well-populated area. It is probably Athelstan's head, carved in stone, above the north door of the parish church of St. Mary.

The arch over the south-east doorway is the most prominent remaining feature of the church, which the Normans built on the slight eminence that forms the town centre. The oldest part of the main structure of the present building is the thirteenth-century tower, paid for by Alicia de Mohun, who died in 1257 and to whom there is a memorial in the church. Most of the gargoyles are original, but the stone parapet replaces the one dating from the sixteenth century, whose stones crumbled.

In the Middle Ages, the Cistercians established an abbey at the confluence of the Axe and the Yarty. There they built a monastic church, 280 feet long. Only a few scattered pieces of masonry remain to outline the site. You can see these traces, if you walk along the footpath between the railway and the River Axe.

The Cistercian brothers left a more enduring mark on Axbridge by establishing it as a major wool town, a reputation that was revived in the late eighteenth century, when one of the citizens, Thomas Whitty, started making carpets. Although the Axminster looms were sold to Wilton in 1835 and although it is only recently that the industry has returned to Devon, the name of Axminster is synonymous with carpets. Thomas Whitty's factory behind the church, in Silver Street, was burnt down in 1827, but his house remains. It is a pleasing two-storey, bow-windowed building, which now serves as the town's Law Chamber.

Axminster was a Royalist stronghold during the Civil War and most of the merchants' houses were burnt down by the Parliamentarians. This means that there are no buildings here of any great antiquity or note apart from the church and the George Hotel near by it. This was established as a coaching inn on the London to Plymouth road.

Now, if you go west out of Axminster along the A35T, you will pass its mid-nineteenth century equivalent: a magnificent, Gothic station building, created in 1859 for the South Western railway running between Salisbury and Exeter.

Barrington 389182
Although well to the east of the area, Barrington (on the B3168 between Curry Rivel and Ilminster) is included in this survey because it lies on the edge of the ancient hunting forest of Neroche, which included a sizeable part of the Blackdown Hills. Barrington is an attractive village of thatched stone-built cottages. Barrington Court is now owned by the National Trust and so open to the public on certain days in the week. It is an attractive two-storey house built for Lord Daubeny in 1514 out of the local, golden stone from Ham Hill, south of Ilminster.

Beckford Bridge 265015
It is well worth seeking out this single-arched, medieval, pack-horse bridge, which crosses the Yarty between Membury and Dalwood. It is no longer in use and stands a little to the north of the present road bridge.

Blackborough 095094
Blackborough church stands high on a wooded ridge. It is an unusually austere nineteenth-century building, erected for the Earl of Egremont, who shared the nearby Blackborough House with the incumbent. This handsome, Italianate, double villa is now used for community purposes.

Bodmiscombe 109098
A tiny hidden hamlet has grown up where the St. John's

Hospitallers established a cell for both men and women on land given to the order by Henry Fitzwilliam of Sheldon (q.v.). The larger of the two farms in the valley is said to have been built round the site of that original cell.

Broadhembury 103047

The thatched cottages, renovated in 1900, which flank the street between the church and the river, make this one of the most picturesque and frequently visited Devon villages. They were originally built to form an estate village in the early seventeenth century, when Edward Drewe, Sergeant-at-Law to Queen Elizabeth I, built his great house nearby on lands acquired after the Dissolution of Dunkeswell Abbey (q.v.). The church dates from the fifteenth century and two medieval buildings stand close by it: Church Gate, which was probably a Priest's House, and the inn, now known as The Drewe Arms. Augustus Montague Toplady, author of the hymn, 'Rock of Ages,' was vicar of Broadhembury from 1768 -1778.

Burlescombe 075167 (OS Sheet 181)

This village on the Somerset Devon border was once served by both canal and railway. Now although the railway line is part of the national network, the village has lost its station, a fact which would surely have annoyed the novelist R.D. Blackmore who wrote some doggerel verses praising the cutting of the White Ball tunnel to the north-west. You can find a copy of his lines in the hill-top church, built of stone from the nearby quarry at Westleigh (q.v.) and faced with limestone from Beer in Devon and Ham Hill in Somerset. Part of the original screen set up during the reign of Henry Vll is still in place.

Canonsleigh Abbey 068173 (OS Sheet 181)

A public footpath runs through Canonsleigh Farm past the ivy-covered ruins of the Abbey, once occupied by a community of Augustinian canonesses, who settled here in the twelfth century. Beyond these ecclesiastical ruins there are the remains of a mill, and the grassed-over track, which once took the stone down from the quarries to the canal wharf.

Castlefields, Wellington Hill 137172
This nature reserve, managed by the Somerset Trust for Nature Conservation, covers 25 acres of the north-facing slopes of the Blackdown Hills adjoining the Wellington monument (q.v.). It comprises an ancient woodland as well as acid grassland, bracken and scrub. Both woods and pasture reflect a continuous traditional management, the Tithe map of 1839 showing little divergence from the present land use.

Chard 324084
Partly because of its very active local history society and its flourishing museum, the industrial history of this still lively little town has been well interpreted for the visitor by means of town trails. By the beginning of the nineteenth century, the wool trade, which for centuries had been the basis of the town's prosperity, began to decline. At the same time the Luddite riots in the Midlands forced the lace manufacturers to seek another location. They came south and by 1830 were employing over fifteen hundred people in the lace works of Chard. The old woollen mills were enlarged and adapted, the machinery being driven by steam.

The Guildhall, where Fore Street and High Street meet, was built in the Tuscan style. A market was on the ground floor level with the Town Hall above it, and the whole edifice reflects the industrial and agricultural prosperity of the town in the 1830s, when it was erected. So does the George Hotel, also built in the Tuscan style. It stands across the road from the Guildhall and has a magnificent four-column porch.

The lace industry in Chard was completely finished by the end of World War II, but two of the mills, both consisting of five storeys, are still standing. However, the Snowdon Collar works, just off the High Street, has been in operation since 1890 and continues to flourish. So textiles still have a part to play in the life of the town.

To the north towards Crimchard, the old rope walk was the scene of agricultural machinery works from 1880 to the 1950s. The site has now been rebuilt as a housing estate, retaining the pleasing proportions of its original use. Crimchard House nearby is an imposing two-storeyed building with mullioned windows. It was once the home of the Wheadons, whose wealth came from their business as wool dyers.

To the east of the Guildhall, in Fore Street, there are several ancient buildings, including a house built in 1583 with an impressive three-storey porch. In 1671 it became the town's grammar school. In this same street you will also find a fine set of Georgian houses and an early Victorian seven-bay house, originally built as an hotel and now used by Lloyd's Bank. According to Pevsner, the most interesting building in Chard stands to the west of the George Hotel. It comprises a group of late Elizabethan houses and forms the Court House, which again boasts a fine three-storey porch.

One of Chard's most famous citizens was John Stringfellow, a lace-making engineer, who was to build the first heavier-than-air flying machine. His house still stands in the High Street to the west of the Guildhall and you can learn about his life and work in the museum on the opposite side of the road. It is open from May to September.

Chardstock 309045

The most interesting building in this most attractive small village is the George Inn, which was originally the Church House, where parish meetings were held. It is a low, thatched, early medieval cruck-beamed construction its interior dominated by a massive hearth-lintel that spans the whole length of the building.

Churchinford 214125
A remote hamlet in a tangle of Blackdown lanes to the west of Brown Down by Robin Hood Butts (q.v.), reported to be the site of a pixie market.

Clayhidon 162157
A tiny hill-top, quintessential Blackdown village, made up of the church, the inn, the old vicarage and a cluster of houses perched on the edge of an escarpment falling east to a tributary of the Culm.

Coldharbour Mill 065124 (OS Sheet 181)
One of the few surviving Devon woollen mills, Coldharbour is still operational, although spinning and weaving are only carried on in a small way and mostly for the instruction of visitors. In its present form, the mill was established in 1797 and continued in full operation until well into the twentieth century. It is now open to the public during the summer months.

Combe St. Nicholas 302112
The medieval church of St. Nicholas contains the remains of a Norman doorway and part of a fifteenth century rood screen. Bronze Age remains have been found at Combe Beacon to the north (297124)

Cotleigh 205023
This small village, to the west of Stockland Hill, may well have been settled by Celtic Christian missionaries. The church was originally dedicated to St. Petroc, who came from South Wales to the south-west of England in the sixth century .

Cricket St. Thomas 373085

Best known for its wild life park and as the setting for the TV series 'To the Manor Born,' Cricket House to the east of the church is well worth visiting for the fine setting of this magnificent mansion built for Admiral Hood, in the first decade of the nineteenth century, on the site of an earlier mansion.

Cullompton 022073 (OS Sheet 192)

On the western outskirts of the Blackdowns, the town of Cullompton still retains signs of the prosperity which the wool trade brought to it in the Middle Ages. Chief among these is the great church. Its tower, one hundred and twenty feet high, carries elaborate pinnacles; but although this must be the first feature to capture your attention, it was, in fact, built in the years immediately preceding the Reformation, a century or so after the main body of the church had been completed. Inside, the greatest glory is an eleven-bay rood screen whose graceful fans support a crest carved with a motif of entwined vines.

Despite a series of fires in the town, culminating in July 1839, when over a hundred houses were burnt down, there are still traces of fine domestic architecture, made possible by the wealth of the wool trade. The grandest mansion in Fore Street is Walronds bought in 1605 by a lawyer, John Peyers. It is framed by a Victorian archway and consists of a three-storey building with wings of two storeys, its most outstanding feature being the large mullioned windows.

Cullompton is a good place to explore. If you enter the archways off the main street, you will find yourself in narrow alleys linking a maze of small courts.

Culmstock 103137

A railway used to run beside the Culm and traces of it can be seen to the north of the bridge, where the inn still carries a railway sign. Soap used to be made in the southern part of the village and was carried by packhorses over the Culm *en route* for Exeter. The church stands on a slight hill also to the south. It houses a Pre-Reformation velvet cope kept on display. The material is covered in delicate embroidery, depicting saints, apostles and martyrs who surround the angels clustered round the Virgin. R.D. Blackmore's father was vicar here and Culmstock, under the guise of *Perlycross* is the location for one of his minor novels, which takes that fictional name for its title.

Culmstock Beacon 110150

High above Culmstock village, on the south-western edge of the Blackdown Ridge, a small circular building stands on the edge of the hill. It was put up in the sixteenth century to protect the beacon fire from the weather.

Dalwood 248005 (OS Sheet 192)

The Tuckers' Arms, which stands on the old green near the church, is most probably of medieval construction. The ceiling in the bar suggests that it may once have been an early hall-type building, later divided into two storeys. There is a general belief that it was originally built as a dwelling place for the builders of the original church, for many centuries a chapelry of Stockland to the north. Loughwood chapel (q.v.) is in the southern part of Dalwood parish.

Dumpdon Hill 176040

This splendidly sited Iron Age enclosure, standing above the Otter, provides a marvellous height from which to view the south-western stretches of the Blackdown. Beneath its southern, wooded slopes, there is a water meadow managed as a nature reserve by the Devon Wildlife Trust.

Dunkeswell 142078
Dunkeswell village, standing high above Mudford River, has been a settlement at least since Saxon times. The church dates from the thirteenth century and was one of those like Cotleigh (q.v.) originally dedicated to Petroc the Celtic missionary.

Dunkeswell Abbey 144107
A gate house is all that is left of the abbey built by the Cistercians at the beginning of the thirteenth century. The remaining fragmentary ruins surround a nineteenth century church built on the site of the conventual chapel . Inside it, diagrams explaining the original lay out of the abbey are displayed.

Dunkeswell airfield 135075
On a plateau above Dunkeswell village there was an American airfield during the Second World War. Its adaption to modern commercial uses is still a matter of intense controversy, many people fearing the results of a greatly increased traffic-flow in the area.

Five Fords 083136 (OS Sheet 181)
A footbridge crosses the Culm between Uffculme and Culmstock, where the meandering river runs back on itself to form a complete circle before taking a slightly less convoluted course to the east.

Fivehead 354229
Lying somewhere to the east of the Blackdown area, Fivehead is included here because of its ancient connection with the Forest of Neroche. The village lies to the south of the ridge covered by the A378. To the north of that main road, in the woods overlooking the Somerset levels, there is an R.S.P.B. reserve which includes a hide from which you can watch a heronry.

Forches Corner 183172

This crossroads marks the Devon/Somerset border on the eastern edge of the Blackdown ridge above Wellington. It gets its macabre name from the gallows that once stood here. It is traditionally believed to be the place where the Saxons finally defeated the Celts of Wessex.

Forde Abbey 364052

Although this Dorset abbey lies well to the east of the Blackdowns it has had an important part to play in the history of the hills. In the Middle Ages, the powerful and wealthy Cistercian monastery that was founded here in the mid-twelfth century owned much land in the Blackdowns. After the Reformation it continued the connection with the Blackdowns. In the seventeenth-century, it was bought by Edmund Prideaux, Attorney General to Oliver Cromwell, and the Duke of Monmouth stayed here during his progress through the west country in 1680.

It is open to the public on Wednesdays, Sundays and Bank Holiday afternoons from mid-March to mid-October. The Abbey gardens, which are well worth visiting on their own account and which enable the visitor to appreciate the general architecture of the house, are open to the public daily throughout the year.

Gaunsey's Tower 102095 (OS Sheet 192)

In the nineteenth century, John Gurnsey, a wealthy bachelor, lived at Bodiscombe (q.v.) where he entertained many lady friends, some of whom he ensconced in the two-storey folly, which he built on the neighbouring hill-top. Locally known as Gaunsey's Tower and so marked on the O.S. Map, it fell down in the 1950s. However, there are still some remains to see, if you take the footpath through the woods to the west of Blackborough (q.v.). From that site there is a magnificent view to the east of Bodiscombe valley.

Hembury 114032 (OS Sheet 192)

Claimed as one of the finest prehistoric hill-top enclosures in the south-west, Hembury's earthworks date from the Iron Age; yet there is archaeological evidence to show that Neolithic settlers once occupied this hill-top, where thousands of years later Roman legions encamped. The public footpath from the A373 will bring you to the west gateway of the fort; alternatively you can approach it by the minor road from Dunkeswell (q.v.) which runs along the ridge of the hill to the north of the enclosure.

Hemyock 135134

In the heart of the Blackdown Hills by the Culm River, the little town of Hemyock has grown up around the industrialisation of dairy products. The first butter factory in the west of England was started here in 1886, and apart from a short spell in the winter of 1975/6, butter making has continued to be the town's main industry and focal point. For the visitor however, it is not the factory but a little monument in the centre of the town which is Hemyock's most distinguishing feature. It takes the form of a wrought iron memorial, gaily painted and set up to mark the reigns of Victoria and Edward VII and to commemorate the end of the Boer War in 1902.

This monument stands at a road junction close to the castle, the thirteenth-century church (much restored in 1768) and the Catherine Wheel Inn, on whose walls the history of the Popham family, who were the local landowners, is displayed. The Pophams supported the Parliamentarians during the Civil War and used Hemyock Castle as a place to confine Royalist prisoners. Because of that, Charles II after the Restoration, ordered that Hemyock Castle be slighted. It was probably then that the walls were breached, much of the stone work no doubt going into local building works. Now all that is left of the fortified manor house, crenelated in 1380, is part of the curtain wall and fragments of six towers including the entrance arch. The castle is open from 2 -5 p.m. on Bank Holidays from Easter to the end of August.

Holcombe Rogus 057190 (OS Sheet 181)

The two most interesting buildings in this attractive village are the Tudor Court, home of the Bluett family from 1430 - 1858 (their specially built Jacobean pew still stands in the fourteenth century church); and the former priest's house, dating from the latter part of the sixteenth century and now in the hands of the Landmark Trust.

Holman Clavell Inn 222161

This public house at the eastern edge of the Blackdown ridge gets its strange name from the great holly-beam lintel above the hearth.

Honiton 164007 (OS Sheet 192)

Honiton, which grew up from a Roman posting station, was to become a town renowned for lace making. The industry began here in the early Middle Ages but it was not until the fifteenth-century when Protestant refugees from the continent settled here that Honiton lace took on its own distinguished characteristics. The various intricate designs of Honiton lace are now all on display in the Lace Museum, housed in the former chapel of All Hallows in the High Street. Elegant two-storey Georgian houses line that wide street, which was formerly part of the main turnpiked thoroughfare, which followed the course of the old Roman road. An elegant castellated toll-house, whose barrier gates are still intact, stands by the A35T to the south-east of the town.

Kentisbeare 068081 (OS Sheet 192)

E.M. Delafield, who lived at Croyle (068095) to the north of this village immortalised the area in her *Diary of a Provincial*

Lady. She lived here from 1923 until her death twenty years later, and was visited in the last months of her life by her friend, Kate O' Brien. E.M. Delafield was buried in Kentisbeare church, which also contains a memorial on the north wall, in the form of a quatrain by Sir Walter Scott. The great novelist fashioned those lines as a tribute to his cousin, George Scott, who was rector here from 1828 to 1830, when he died from scarlet fever, being then twenty-six years old.

Literary interests apart, this church is well worth visiting for the splendour of its ten-bay rood screen, which stretches across the nave and south aisle. It was made by craftsmen from Tavistock Abbey during the reign of Henry VII, who probably stayed in the medieval church house while they were carrying out the work. This building, now known as Priesthall, still stands beside the churchyard.

Lickham Bottom 125124
Anyone who is interested in the flora and fauna of wetlands should try and arrange a visit to this reserve owned by the Devon Wildlife Trust. Its particular features are a covering of bog myrtle and the carefully nurtured alder buckthorn, which attracts the acid-yellow brimstone butterflies.

Longbridge 255055
This bridge on the old Exeter to London coach road carries a notice, placed there in 1770, warning anyone who might wilfully damage it that they are liable to be transported for life.

Loughwood Chapel 253993 (OS Sheet 192)
The National Trust is the owner of the site of this ancient Baptist chapel which stands on farmland in the parish of Dalwood (q.v.). The chapel was formed in the mid-sixteenth century from a cottage remote enough to enable the minister and his congregation to escape the savage persecution of the

non-conformists that occurred after the Restoration. Services are still held here and the whole building retains its character from the days when a sermon might go on for an hour or more and the spring-fed tank beneath the pulpit was regularly used for baptism by total immersion.

Luppit 169068
This remote village is worth visiting for its beautiful, remote hill-side setting and for the Norman, possibly Saxon, font in its fourteenth century church. This is one of the most interesting fonts in the country on account of the elaborate carvings on its four faces (See Chapter 3 p 34).

Membury Castle 285028
A hill-fort on the high ground between the Yarty and the Axe, Membury Castle is about half-a-mile to the south-east of Membury church. The footpath from Passland Farm to Chapplecroft Farm runs east beneath the southern edge of the fort. Alternatively it is possible to enter the enclosure by taking the footpath that runs north from the same starting point and climbing up to the earthworks surrounding the northern aspect of the enclosure.

Membury Court 265037
Holiday accommodation is available in this sixteenth century farmhouse, one of whose barns has been built round the site of a fourteenth century chapel. Two windows of the original structure remain, the piscina is still intact, and there are traces of a wide upper gallery projecting towards the sanctuary.

Monkton 187032
The A30 runs right through this village on the east bank of the Otter. The garage on the western side of the road shows unmistakable signs of its original use as a smithy; and the church, which stands close by it, has a window designed by

Burne-Jones and executed by William Morris' company.

Neroche (Castle) 272158

These vast earthworks, on the edge of a wooded hill in the centre of the ancient hunting forest of Neroche, date from the middle of the eleventh century, the outer banks being of Saxon origin. In 1067, when William the Conqueror's half-brother, Robert of Mortain, took control of the area, an elaborate fort was constructed, culminating in a conical motte at the highest point of the hill. Later this was used as a beacon site. The area is now owned by the Forestry Commission, who have undertaken extensive broad leaf planting round the site. Visitors are welcome and there is ample car parking space.

Northay Barrow 281114

To the west of the lane about a mile to the north of Whitestaunton (q.v.), this solitary burial mound dates from the Bronze Age.

Offwell 195996

The thirteenth century church at the centre of this village is set on a small hill traversed by a beautifully cobbled path. Its chief treasure is a portion of a sixteenth century rood screen, brought here after the demolition of the original church of St. Mary Major in Exeter. To the west of the church, a nature reserve has been created out of the pleasure garden laid out in the mid-nineteenth century by Dr. Copplestone then vicar of the parish. A hundred years later his seventy-five acres were completely clogged by rhododendrons and these had to be cleared before any natural habitat could re-emerge.

Otterford 223143

An isolated, largely Victorian church stands to the north of Royston Water and serves the scattered farms of Brown Down and Churchinford.

Pitminster 221191

There are some splendid sixteenth and seventeenth-century effigies of members of the Coles family in this much restored medieval church.

Prior's Park Wood 215174

A footpath runs through the woods that cover the eastern slopes of Blagdon Hill. It runs past the stonework of impressive Gothic waterworks, dating from the time when Blackdown landowners organised their own water supply.

Poundisford Park 225202

This Tudor mansion was built on an unusual H-plan in the reign of Henry VIII on land which was once a part of the Bishop of Winchester's deer park. Poundisford Lodge to the north (224207) was built about the same time. It was originally leased to Roger Hill, father of William Hill, who made substantial interior alterations to Poundisford Park in 1570.

Quants 189176

A ruined farmhouse gives its name to this thirty-four acre nature reserve managed by the Somerset Trust for Nature Conservation . The reserve includes part of Buckland Wood just below Forches Corner (q.v.), so combining ancient woodland with scrub and rough grazing heathland. The footpath climbing uphill through the wood from the small car park passes the elaborate stonework marking the entrance to tunnels connected with an old water system .

Robin Hood Butts 237128

A group of tumuli to the west of the B3170, which runs along the Brown Down ridge. They are all on private land, the most visible barrow being to the north of the lane that runs west of the ridge to Churchinford. The barrows get their name from the dents at the top of each one, supposedly made by the quoits which Robin Hood and Little John hurled at each other. Local folk-lore had it that the mounds were the burial places of Oliver Cromwell's soldiers.

Rosemary Lane 157146
The tiny settlement beside this steep lane, running between the River Culm and Clayhidon, includes one of the original chapels of the Blackdown Mission founded in the 1860s.

Sheldon 120086 (OS Sheet 192)
There are no traces now of the four farms, which once formed the nucleus of this hill-top village. Their fields have been built over since the nineteenth century; nevertheless the countryside around Sheldon, and in particular its ancient woodlands, still retains some echoes of the lands, which together with the parish church, were given to the Bishop of Exeter in 1243.

Spiceland 083142
This Quaker Meeting House, built in 1670 and rebuilt in 1815, stands in the garden of a private house to the north-west of Culmstock (q.v.). The Trust Deed bequeathing the building for a religious purpose is dated the sixteenth of the seventh month 1683 and grants that 'the people of God called Quakers ... or any other that should incline thereto should have the right to make use of the said house and the materials therein as a free and open place for them to assemble.' The Meeting House is still in use and furnished with its early nineteenth century pine benches. Visitors are welcome.

Stockland 245045
This is one of the most interesting of the Blackdown villages on account of its many and varied ancient buildings. The most extreme example of these is the tiny, cob-walled, thatched church-ale or cider-house by the south-west corner of the

churchyard. This building, restored in 1983, is probably older than the present church, built in the fifteenth century and standing on a slight eminence where a Saxon church once replaced a pagan shrine.

Stockland Great Castle 223026
This vast encampment stands on private ground on the ridge of Stockland Hill. From the lane, however, it is possible to appreciate the very deep ditch and high earthworks (now wooded) that surround the enclosure.

Stockland Little Castle 230035
A clearly defined circular hill-top enclosure. This hill fort or cattle pound has not been excavated, but it is thought to be of Celtic origin.

Stoke St. Mary 265223
This is a village of many attractive, early buildings, including Furse Cottage, the thatched house at its centre, which dates from the sixteenth century. It was enlarged in 1658 by Thomas Furse, a lime burner, who carved his name over the door. Stoke Court, which dates from the early seventeenth century, has a two-storeyed porch.

Taunton 228248
The best way to appreciate Somerset's county town is by taking a walk along the banks of the Tone from Firepool (by the railway station) where the Bridgwater and Taunton Canal meets the river, past the County cricket ground and the Brewhouse Theatre to the gardens around the Castle Museum, which houses the main collection of artefacts connected with the county.

As for the Taunton churches: your eye will naturally have been caught by the 163-feet high tower of St. Mary Magdalene, rebuilt in 1862 by the eminent Victorian architect, Gilbert

Scott, who kept strictly to the original, medieval form. Inside, the church has unusual double aisles, the northernmost arcade dating from the late thirteenth century. Above the nave and south porch, the carved and painted fifteenth century ceiling has been carefully restored. The best way to approach this church is along Hammet Street, designed in the eighteenth century as a carriage road to the church. That road runs off the eastern side of Fore Street, below the early eighteenth century, red-brick Market House, which now virtually forms a traffic island.

As a centre of nonconformity, Taunton has many interesting chapels as well as several other, mainly nineteenth-century churches. Look out particularly for the Friends Meeting House in Bath Place, the narrow walk-way off the pedestrianised High Street; the former Wesleyan octagon chapel, standing in Middle Street, just north of the town bridge; and the Unitarian and Free Christian chapel, where the young Coleridge preached. It is in Mary Street at the northern end of the High Street.

A cattle and produce market is held in the market hall by the railway station on Saturdays.

Thurlbear 266211
There are two Norman arcades, dating from the early twelfth century, in this splendidly situated and isolated church.

Thurlbear Wood 273213
A Somerset Trust nature reserve, part of which is a woodland Site of Special Scientific Interest. Thurlbear Wood is notable for its rich limestone glades which attract a wide range of butterflies as well as an abundance of ground flora associated with ancient woodlands.

Uffculme 068127

The sloping triangular 'square' of this village still retains traces of the twelfth century shambles. There is a glorious fifteenth-century screen stretching across the nave of the much-restored parish church, which also contains the elaborate tomb of the seventeenth-century William Walrond. For centuries, his family and the other local landowners grew rich on the wool trade, vestiges of which can be seen at the mill at nearby Coldharbour (q.v.).

Wellington 141209 (OS Sheet 181)

The Duke of Wellington chose to take the name of this small Somerset town because of its near approximation to his family name of Wellesley. There is no other close connection and the main interest for the town's visitors today lies in its more recent architectural history and in the vestiges of its long connection with the cloth trade and the textile industry.

Wellington grew in prosperity and expanded greatly from about 1880 to the end of the Edwardian era. This expansion is marked by the work of two architects: Edwin Thomas Howard and his son Ernest Tom. Both men made use of the local brick, which they adorned with stone dressing, terracotta panels and a wealth of idiosyncratic detail. Their own home was at Number 8 High Path to the north of the town centre. You can see other examples of their work in Station Road, Waterloo Road (note the Gothic doorway of Number 58) and Wellesley Park, where Number 29 (Sunnycroft) is acclaimed as the Howards' masterpiece.

Much of the wealth that enabled this expansion to take place came from the textile works. These are now defunct although the remains of one mill remains in a derelict and dilapidated state, the late twentieth-century recession having defeated the plan to turn it into a thriving industrial estate for individual firms and craft workers. Now the more lively reminder of Wellington's cloth trade is provided by the basins, which form part of a park in the north of the town. The parish church, much restored but with some medieval features remaining, contains a carving of one of the priests who served here in the fourteenth century and a monument to Lord Chief Justice Popham, who presided over the trials of Sir Walter Raleigh and the Guy Fawkes conspirators. The judge has his wife at his side and their children kneeling around them.

Wellington Monument 135173
Standing on National Trust ground, on the height of the Blackdown ridge, the monument erected to the memory of the Duke of Wellington is a familiar landmark to travellers driving along the M5 beneath it. If you climb up inside this triangular tower (keys and a torch are available from Monument Farm 137169) you can look south over much of the Blackdown Hills.

Westleigh 061169 (OS Sheet 181)
For centuries, this small settlement which grew around Canonsleigh Abbey (q.v.) has been dominated by the quarries which originally provided the stone for much of the building and nearly all the lime-burning in the Blackdown Hills. For some years the stone was carried away by canal and rail. It is now used for roadstone and carted to its destination by heavy lorries.

Whitestaunton 281105
A sheltered village with a long history. A Roman villa was discovered here in 1840 when road works were being done; and there are traces of Celtic earthworks beside the footpath to the north of the church. The church itself contains a fluted Norman font, a stone screen and a few Tudor bench ends.

Widcombe Wildlife Park 218158

The park and gardens surrounding the early nineteenth century Widcombe House are open to the public from April to October. The garden and its artificial lake were laid out in the Edwardian era and include a collection of rare shrubs and trees which have now reached maturity. The parkland contains some unusual birds and animals brought in by the present owners, Michael and Stella Peacock. For further information call 01823 421268.

Wolford Chapel 136053

John Graves Simcoe, the first Lieutenant Governor of Upper Canada, who died in Exeter in October 1806, is buried in this chapel which he built three years previously. It stands in the grounds of Wolford Lodge which he built in the 1880s and which was to retain the family seat until 1923. The chapel, which is thought to stand on the site of an ancient abbey, was designated Ontario property in 1966. It is now maintained and made accessible to the public during daylight hours by the Ontario Heritage Foundation. Further information is available from Ontario House. 21 Knightsbridge, London SW1 7LY. Tel 0171 245 1222.

More books on Somerset from Ex Libris Press:

CHEDDAR VALLEY RAILWAY WALK
by Douglas Kidder
112 pages; Illustrated;
ISBN 0 948578 44 0; Price £5.95

COLLIERS WAY:
History and Walks in the Somerset Coalfield
by Peter Collier
160 pages; Illustrated;
ISBN 0 948578 43 2; Price £6.95

GEOLOGY OF SOMERSET
by Peter Hardy
224 pages; Illustrated;
ISBN 0 948578 42 4; Price £9.95

THE MENDIPS
by Robin & Romy Williams
176 pages; Illustrated;
ISBN 0 948578 76 9; Price £7.95

MENDIP RAMBLES
12 Circular Walks on Mendip
by Peter Wright
80 pages; Illustrated;
ISBN 0 948578 33 5; Price £4.50

THE SOMERSET LEVELS by Robin & Romy Williams
176 pages; Illustrated;
ISBN 0 948578 38 6; Price £7.95

WELLS: *An Historical Guide* by Martin Langley
104 pages; Illustrated;
ISBN 0 948578 24 6; Price £5.95

WEST MENDIP WAY by Derek Moyes
112 pages; Illustrated;
ISBN 0 948578 45 9; Price £5.95

WHERE WILTSHIRE MEETS SOMERSET
20 Best Walks in the Country around Bath,
Bradford on Avon, Trowbridge, Westbury,
Warminster and Frome
by Roger Jones
128 pages; Illustrated;
ISBN 0 948578 94 7; Price £5.95

Books from Ex Libris Press are available through
your local bookshop or direct from the publisher,
post-free, on receipt of net price
EX LIBRIS PRESS, 1 The Shambles,
Bradford on Avon, Wiltshire, BA15 1JS
Tel/Fax 01225 863595
E mail: rogjones37@hotmail.com